Sell Retail Now!

A Salon Owner's Guide to Wealth

By Jeff Grissler & Eric Ryant

"Jeff Grissler has been contributing to this industry for many years and now he compiles his best work. Retailing in no longer a luxury. Selling retail is now a necessity to stay in business. This book will show you exactly how to stay creative and sell retail too.

Very soon, the only salons open will be those that understand the art of selling retail products. Jeff Grissler will teach you how to do it best. Buy this book and your reward is that your salon will be more profitable and you will earn more money.

Jeff had put on the pages precisely what you need to do to increase retail sales. Start selling now by implement these ideas into your company. Learn what most of the big boys are doing today to increase profit.

The largest money pit in salons today is the lack of retail sales. Jeff Grissler shows you the way to increase retailed and how to keep it there. This is the future of beauty in action. This is what I teach.

The first thing I share with the salon I consult is selling retail is a must. In order to maintain you must sell and increase retail sales and know how to position it. This book makes it easy for you to do both and more. Get this book and stay in business making money."

— *Geno Stampora*
Master Educator, NAHA Hall of Leaders Member

Books by Jeff Grissler and Eric Ryant
Ready Set Go Publishing, LLC

Ready, Set, Go! The Start-Up Guide for Opening, Remodeling, & Running a Successful Barbershop
© 2012 Jeff Grissler and Eric Ryant. All Rights Reserved.

Find other Ready Set Go series books on www.salonresourceguide.com

First edition.

Published in the U.S. by Ready Set Go Publishing, LLC
215 Pascal Street
Fort Collins Colorado 80524

Printed in the United States of America

ISBN: 978-0-9855802-1-6

About the Authors

2012 Edition

Jeff Grissler has been where you are and understands the inner workings of the hair industry and what leads to success as a salon owner. As a business owner himself, he knows the business landscape and what owners can expect and guides them to success. Jeff is a partner of and the National Sales Manager for Quest Resources—one of the hair industry's leading financing companies for furniture and equipment. His career in finance actually began on Wall Street and he has been involved in the multimillion dollar hair and beauty industry for over 20 years. Jeff has financed over 15,000 salons and barbershops to help them open their doors or complete their remodeling project through creative financing strategies. Published in many hair and beauty trade magazines, Jeff is setting a new business standard in the hair industry as we see it today. Jeff has a portfolio of over $600 million dollars in salon financing and a network of over 150 manufacturers, distributors, and vendors. A gifted businessman and consultant, Jeff prides himself on his networking ability to bring people together to share new ideas and explore partnerships and marketing techniques. Through his skilled negotiations, he has convinced the banking industry to lift restrictions from the hair and beauty industry. He has also negotiated contracts and leases with salon owners, spa owners, distributors, manufacturers, and banking management.

Jeff was born in New York City before moving to the Jersey Shore. He was a New York City fireman for 15+ years and served during 911. Jeff now resides in Wilmington, NC, with his wife, Coleen, and their three children—Kaytlyn, JT, and Juliana Rose. Jeff offers consulting services to current salon owners and to those who have ownership of a salon, nail, or spa business in their near-term or future career plans. To reach Jeff, you can contact him directly at jgrissler@questrs.com.

Eric Ryant is a beauty industry entrepreneur with over 30 years of experience in space planning and design for salons. No stranger to the hair and beauty industry, Eric spent many years developing new designs and space plans, getting involved in every facet of the industry. Since the 1980s, Eric has imported salon and barbering furniture from many countries, such as Italy, Germany, Holland, and China, bringing in the latest trends and styles for the U.S. market. Prior to writing this book, Eric owned several successful businesses, all involved in the hair and beauty industry, from a small chain of beauty stores to a cabinet manufacturing facility. He has also collaborated with companies such as Sally Beauty Supply, L'Oreal and The Nailco Group.

Eric's vision is to help business owners to create their dreams with a cost-effective business model and ensure that they stay within budget for the long haul. As part of his successful career, he now teaches and consults with other organizations on how to achieve the same success. Eric can be reached at ericryant@gmail.com.

Acknowledgements

Jeff Grissler

You never really understand how important your friends and family are until you take on a large project. My wife, Coleen, was my sounding board and always had insightful feedback. I can't tell you how much I appreciated her support and encouragement. My children, Kaytlyn, JT, and Julianna are always an inspiration and fill my life with joy. I also can never forget to mention mom and dad for always believing in me and never doubting my dreams and sometimes crazy ideas. To Jason Frye at Teakettle Junction Productions for his writing and editing help. To Robin Krauss at Linden Design for his expert help putting the book together.

Eric Ryant

First and foremost, I want to thank my mother, Cynthia. She has always been the backbone of the family and even though I don't express it as much as I should, I do love her dearly. To my father, Harvey, who passed many years ago, thanks for watching over me. To my children, Chase, Kendall, and Sloane, just know that anything is possible and writing this second book is proof again that anything is possible when you put your mind to it.

INTRODUCTION

There's no debating it – the beauty industry is a multi-billion dollar industry. Billion, not million. It's booming and, even though the economy has suffered in other sectors, in the beauty industry, things have stayed steady.

Why? It's simple, it comes down to vanity. People want to look better and feel better. They want to be perceived as beautiful by themselves and others. They want to look younger and more attractive than those around them.

Think about it: the economy is struggling to rebound, corporations are cutting jobs and small businesses pop up for one year and disappear the next, periods of unemployment have gotten longer and the competition for jobs has become tougher. What's the one thing that could give a job seeker an edge over another job seeker? What's the one thing that could help lift someone from an emotional and financial depression?

Beauty.

If they look better, they feel better, if they feel better, they perform better in job interviews. Attractive people exude confidence and charisma and the people around them believe they can get the job done. Beauty can give them the edge over another job candidate. Beauty can give them some self-assurance that will help pull them out of a depressed, woe-is-me mindset.

So how can you enter this multi-billion dollar industry, help people achieve their beauty goals and make a good living for yourself? By opening a salon. But if you want to make a great living for yourself and build your salon into one that you can franchise or sell someday, one that will be a legacy when you walk out the door with a nice retirement nest egg, what do you do?

You open a salon focused on retail.

Retail sales in salons can be a huge revenue stream. They can make you stand out among your competitors, establish you as an authority on beauty, position you as the go-to-resource for all things beautiful, and the salon of choice in your community. Unlike actual physical employees or booth renters, retail is a drama-free moneymaker. Retail products don't show up to work late, bring their boyfriend drama into the salon, create tension among employees or cause any negativity in the salon. Retail simply sits there making you money.

We know what you're thinking – "Opening a salon is hard enough, why would I try to open a retail salon when my clients can get the same shampoo at the grocery store?"

You're right, it's hard to open any business. And you're right, some shampoos, even name brand shampoos, are available at the grocery stores. But you're missing the point. What sets your business apart? Why would your clients buy hair or beauty products from you rather than a grocery store or other retail outlet?

The answer is you.

Your expertise. Your experience. Your drive. Your employees. Your salon. Your in-depth knowledge of what can help your clients reach their beauty goals.

Selling retail, especially in the beauty industry, isn't rocket science. Your clients come to you to look and feel better, they like the way you do their hair (or nails or whatever other services you offer). Your clients come to you looking for product advice. What if instead of sending them (and their money) to another store, you directed them to the product you have on hand? The very one they just used. The one and only product that will deliver the results they need. The one you're going to spend five minutes demonstrating to them and teaching them how to use before they leave your salon.

If you do this – demonstrate a product's use, value and benefits to your client – you can almost guarantee yourself a long-term income from product sales to your client. Once they see you as the authority and resource you are, they'll trust you for their beauty products, and that means more income per client per year.

Let's say you see 20 clients a day and they spend an average of $5 additional dollars each on a retail product in your salon, that would get you $500 extra a week (we're assuming you're open five days). Or $2,000 a month. Or $25,000 a year (we gave you a two week, paid vacation).

What would that extra income cover? Your rent? The mortgage on your house? College tuition for your kids or new car or vacation of a lifetime fund? Would it help you hire another stylist, expand your salon or increase business in some other way?

If a thought about how you could use an additional $25,000 a year popped into your head, this book is for you.

If you want to open a successful salon with a strong retail focus, this book is for you.

TABLE OF CONTENTS

INTRODUCTION

Table of Contents

— For New Salon Owners and Entrepreneurs —

Part I: Are You Ready for Salon Success?

Part II: Getting it Together - Setting Up Your Salon

— Running Your Retail Salon —

Part III: Profit Everywhere You Look

Part IV: Furniture and Fixtures

— The First Year and Beyond —

— PART I —

ARE YOU READY FOR SALON SUCCESS?

CHAPTER 1

Getting Started

"Belief in oneself is one of the most important bricks in building any successful venture."

—Lydia M. Child

Close your eyes and think about one of the earliest flirtations you had with business ownership. Like so many other kids, you probably belonged to some group (scouts, a church or civic group, a club or sports team) that held a car wash fundraiser. Why did you hold a fundraiser? Was it to meet and greet the neighbors? Did washing, drying and waxing a car thrill you? Or did you do it for one simple reason: to make money?

Sometimes you'd count the money at the end of a long day of washing cars and you'd find that you'd exceeded your goals and raised more than enough money; other times there's barely enough to cover the expenses. Why do some car washes succeed while others fail? It's the same question we ask when we see another restaurant, boutique, art gallery or salon open and close within a few months while one street over, business is booming.

Success in business depends on many factors. We've all heard "Location, location, location" in reference to real estate, but it's just as important in business. Can one neighborhood support two fund-raising car washes or four Indian restaurants or another salon offering the exact same services at the same price point? Maybe, but it's quite a gamble to open so near the competition and many areas in the nation don't have the population to support such dense business saturation.

How do you overcome this problem?

By getting noticed.

Think of a car wash manned by enthusiastic kids waving signs and cajoling passers by to get their car washed. Do they stand a better chance of success than the car wash down the road that everyone drives by but no one sees?

By setting yourself apart.

Now think of a car wash stand that offers waxing, vacuuming or interior cleaning. They've set themselves apart and increased their odds of success and (maybe) profitability.

You can do these things with your business. You can make yourself known with targeted advertisements and positive word-of-mouth exposure, and you can set yourself apart by offering a treatment, experience or product the competition doesn't.

The fact that you've picked up this book says that you're committed to growing or establishing your own retail salon. The beauty industry is booming and is only projected to continue to grow. According to the US Department of Labor, personal care and service jobs are slated to grow by 20% from 2008-2018. That's another 1 million jobs added in just a decade.

Perhaps The Wall Street Journal said it best in a July 2012 article, "Why Hairdressers Are Secure: Their Jobs Can't Be Exported." The article says that "jobs that involve assisting or caring for other people… have one thing in common: they aren't easily automated or outsourced." The authors quote a 20-year salon veteran who says, "You can't send people to China or India for a hair cut." As tongue-in-cheek as this statement might be, it's true. Jobs that provide an immediate service and answer a need, especially a need that plays to our own vanity, will never go away.

> **Fact**
>
> Despite the economic times, people are still driven to buy products and services that make them look and feel good.

Why is the beauty industry in the midst of such explosive growth? Several factors contribute, but many of them come down to vanity. We want to look better because when we look better we feel better and when we feel better, well, the world just seems better. We want to look better because the professional job market has become hyper-competitive and job seekers need to look younger and fresher to gain a competitive edge.

That's where you come in.

> **Fact**
>
> The beauty industry is enjoying a continued boom as more people desire to look and feel young and lead healthier lives.

It's your spark, your desire, your drive to help people look great and feel better about themselves that can launch you and your salon to success. Look at this book as a resource for your success. In the following pages you'll find checklists, questions and advice from your fellow professionals that will help you build a salon that delivers satisfaction to your clients, real security to your employees and profits to you, the owner.

CHAPTER 2

What it Takes

"If you hear a voice within you say 'you cannot paint,' then by all means paint, and that voice will be silenced."

—Vincent Van Gogh

Make no mistake, managing a business for someone else is hard work and owning one yourself is even harder, but expanding your salon to include retail, well that opens up a new world of client and customer satisfaction , profit potential and sets your salon apart from the competition.

But to even get to the point of expanding your salon to include retail, you need the salon, and to have the salon, you need to answer a few questions. No matter if you're a veteran salon owner, a manager looking to strike out on your own and open a salon or a beauty school graduate (or near graduate), take a look at these questions and ask yourself if you're ready to start your journey to owning a profitable retail salon.

Fact

600,000 new businesses are founded each year.

1. Do I have experience managing multiple employees?
2. Am I comfortable with the accounting and inventory control a retail salon brings with it?
3. Do I have the basic management skills to run a business?
4. Am I skilled and confident with the computer?
5. Am I a quick learner?
6. Does my current position provide me with benefits and security I am unwilling to risk to achieve my dream of business ownership?
7. Do I have experience with retail ordering, product pricing, product display and product sales?
8. Do I have the ability to educate my employees to successfully sell retail?

9. Can I envision success and get others onboard to help make that vision reality?

10. Do I like the security of working for someone else? Is that more important to me than starting my own salon?

11. Am I committed to doing what it takes to achieve my dream of retail salon ownership?

If you take a closer look at the questions above, you'll see they involve passion, dedication and fundamental business intelligence (FBI). Don't worry if you answered "No" to any or even most of the questions – though you did need to say, "Yes, I am committed to doing what it takes to achieve my dream" – there are plenty of business coaches, classes, small business help centers, mentors and peers to call on for help. We also cover this in great detail in our first book, *Ready, Set, Go! The Start-up Guide for Opening, Remodeling & Running a Successful Beauty Salon.*

For now, we need to look at your answers. If you said that the security and benefits in your current position are too much to give up right now, this book will help you be a bigger part of the team at the salon where you work. When applied properly and in the correct situation, the tools, tips and resources found here can make you a real asset to the salon and push you into new levels of responsibility until you are ready to strike out on your own.

If you've found that you have the desire and motivation to start your salon and retail store, you'll find this book to be the most comprehensive learning guide for getting ready to build a successful retail salon.

One more question: How do you know if you're ready? There are a number of indicators, but take the advice of one stylist/owner who told us how she knew she was ready: "When I had too many clients to handle on my own, even after working a 14-hour day four times a week." If you're there or close to that, you're showing the skills, drive and loyal customer base that you'll need in your own salon.

To help you decide on your next steps, take the test below. Answer honestly and you'll uncover more information about yourself and your ability to own and operate a successful salon.

Please rate these questions 1 to 5 (1 being lowest and 5 highest)

	1	2	3	4	5
1. I seek opportunities all the time.	○	○	○	○	○
2. I look toward the future, not the past.	○	○	○	○	○
3. I am committed to being the best.	○	○	○	○	○
4. I am driven by the needs of the customer.	○	○	○	○	○
5. I have experience working in a retail/sales setting.	○	○	○	○	○
6. I know what products my clients desire and need.	○	○	○	○	○
7. I value employees and I am willing to develop them.	○	○	○	○	○
8. I am tolerant of small tasks.	○	○	○	○	○
9. I do not accept failure.	○	○	○	○	○
10. I am optimistic, but have a realistic outlook.	○	○	○	○	○
11. I have business management experience.	○	○	○	○	○
12. I am decisive and focused.	○	○	○	○	○

Scoring Breakdown:

1. If you scored less than 30 points, we recommend you get a job in a progressive salon in your area. This will help you develop the experience and business know how – as well as help you mature as a professional – you need for business ownership. Revisit the test in a year.

2. If your score is between 30 and 40 points, we recommend you concentrate on your work ethic and take some courses on self-development or business management.

3. If your score is greater than 40 points, you're ready for the next step. There is no guarantee of success, but the opportunity is there. Your drive and determination will help you overcome the obstacles in your way; business courses or business coaching can help take care of the rest.

✓ CHECK IT OUT

Here are some of the main reasons people start their own salon retail businesses:

- To be in control
- To have more freedom
- To create something special
- To feel successful
- To gain recognition
- To feel a sense of accomplishment
- To improve their financial situations
- To build a better future
- To be their own boss
- To focus on a retirement plan

CHAPTER 3

Own a Slice of the Pie

"America is the best place to dream something, design something, start something and build an empire!"

—Anonymous

What's more American than baseball and apple pie? Not much, but owning your own slice of the pie and succeeding because of your hard work would have to be at the top of that list. Working hard, owning your own business and working for yourself have always been staples of American life and an important part of the "American Dream." But what is the American Dream? What does your slice of the pie look like? Is it marriage, two kids, a big house in the suburbs and a dog? Or is it living in the middle of the city, eating fine food, shopping in great boutiques and traveling? Or does it look completely different?

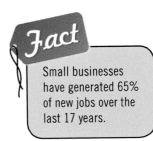

Fact

Small businesses account for nearly half of the employment opportunities in the United States.

For each of us, our ideal slice of pie looks different, but it comes down to this: it's about building a better life for yourself; taking advantage of opportunities to succeed based on your talents, aspirations and abilities; having the things you need and the lifestyle you want.

Many people work to grab their slice the same way you are – business ownership.

While millions of Americans trudge off to work each day in a company that provides the promise of a regular paycheck, job security and a benefits package, millions more aren't content to have someone else control their destiny and limit access to fulfilling their dream. You are among this second group that says, "Damn the security of a corporate job, I'm succeeding on my own terms."

The good news is that success stories from your fellow entrepreneurs are all around. Take a look at these statistics from the Small Business Administration (SBA).

Fact

Small businesses have generated 65% of new jobs over the last 17 years.

In 2009, the recession was in full swing, yet more than a half-million visionaries saw the opportunity for success and stability and opened new businesses. That says something about the power of the American Dream.

But let's look at the last statistic from the SBA. Where do you want your business to fall? In the 70% that lasts two years? The 50% that lasts five years? The 33% that lasts 10 years? The 25% that lasts 15 years or more?

Fact

Seven of 10 new businesses survive at least two years, half at least five years, a third at least 10 years and a quarter for 15 years or more.

That's right, you want to be in the last two categories, the businesses that last a decade or longer.

How do you get there? Hard work, determination and FBI certainly play a part, but to find your success, you'll need a roadmap. That's where knowing your vision and your goals comes in. When you know where you want to end up, you can develop a strong plan to get there. When you clearly see your vision, you know the steps it will take to make it reality.

Take a few minutes to answer the questions below and examine your personal American Dream. We'll call this your personal vision. Keep in mind that your personal vision can change and evolve as you meet your personal and business goals; as the financial, familial and emotional facets of your life change; and as you mature as a person and a business owner. We ask that you revisit these questions every six months to keep them current and to see where you've come from (which is just as important as where you're headed).

Personal Vision

1. Where do I want to be financially within the year? Be specific.

_____

_____

_____

2. How will I reach my financial goals?

_____

_____

3. Three things I want to accomplish for myself this year are:

_____

_____

_____

4. I want to find success in this business because…(be very specific here, why this business, why this industry, what this success will bring you)

_____

_____

_____

5. My personal growth goals for the year are: (examples: to be more compassionate, to become a better listener, to develop public speaking skills)

_____

_____

_____

6. How will I reach these goals?

_____

_____

_____

7. What do I value above all else?

_____

_____

_____

8. What does my perfect day look like?

_____

_____

_____

9. What are three things I am passionate about?

_____

_____

_____

10. How many hours a week do I work?

_____

_____

_____

11. What am I doing to reach that $1,000,000 goal?

_____

_____

_____

Answering these questions honestly can be a little scary, but we want you to know that all new business owners have been afraid for the life of their business and have had to face some tough challenges. Read these multiple choice questions and find the choice that would lead your business to success rather than the other direction.

If you didn't reach your financial goal, what would you do?

○ Throw your hands up?

○ Shut the salon?

○ Scream at anyone who will listen.

○ Look for help through a consultant, your product manufacturer, your accountant, a business coach or a mentor?

If three of your stylists walked out the door of your salon and opened their own shop around the corner, what would you do?

○ Close your salon and join them?

○ Run to the doctor for a bottle of anti-anxiety medicine?

○ Contact a business coach to seek help?

○ Trim expenses until you hire new stylists?

○ A combination of two of these?

If you loose your passion for hair, what should you do?

○ Stop cutting hair and look for a new profession?

○ Go back to school and get motivated?

○ Go to a beauty show to get revived?

If you are not finding enough time to manage the salon, what should you do?

○ Don't worry about it because you hired adults who can manage themselves?

○ Split some of your responsibilities with some of your team?

○ Hire a bookkeeper for paying bills and payroll?

○ Put in some extra hours to get the tedious work done?

CHAPTER 4

Defining Your Dream

"Let the beauty that we love be what we do."

—Rumi

Being able to clearly see your personal vision is only one half of achieving your ultimate goal – business success. Let's take a look at your salon from head to tail and define all of the parts – the services, products, aesthetic, employees, reputation and more – that build a lasting business.

As you work through this chapter, feel free to write in this book (it's yours, after all) or copy, print or download the pages and fill them out. Like with your personal vision, we want you to revisit these questions every six months or every year at the least. This helps you keep your business on track and allows you to revise your mission, goals and standards to reflect the culture, products and services of your salon.

This Is My Dream

My Salon

When I close my eyes and imagine my salon:

- I see: _____

- I hear: _____

- I smell: _____

- I feel: _____

Define each area of your salon

The reception area:

- Looks like: _____

- Makes clients feel: _____
- Sounds like: _____
- Smells like: _____

The stylists' booths:

- Look like (think color, texture, pattern, lighting): _____
- Are arranged/organized: _____
- Make clients feel: _____

Specialized treatment areas (manicure/pedicure, spa and medical spa areas):

- Make clients feel: _____
- Look like: _____
- Smell like: _____
- Sound like: _____

My retail area:

- Is visually appealing because: _____
- Offers products from _____ because: _____
- Is arranged: _____
- Provides clients: _____

My reception area:

- Looks like: _____
- Smells like: _____
- Has: _____
- Makes clients feel safe and comfortable because? _____

- Is warm and welcoming? _____

- Makes clients happy? _____

- Entices clients to spend money on products that will help them achieve their beauty goals? _____

- The furniture in my reception area is: _____

My restrooms/changing rooms:

- Look like: _____

- Make clients feel: _____

- Smell like: _____

- Has: _____

My Employees

Employees of my salon:

- Look: _____

- Say: _____

- Make clients feel: _____

- Do: _____

- Know: _____

- Sell clients _____ because: _____

- Are compensated: _____

- Are on the leading edge of their studies? _____

- Stay ahead of the trends? _____

- Deliver consistent results? _____

- Dress like: _____

- Are cheerful and friendly? _____

My Products

My salon sells:

- _____ hair-care products because: _____

- _____ skin-care products because: _____

- _____ beauty tools because: _____

- _____ cosmetics because: _____

- _____ organic/green products because: _____

My employees:

- Know how to identify up sell opportunities? _____

- Recommend products to _____ clients.

- Convert _____% of recommendations into sales.

- Use the products we sell. _____

- Receive a commission of _____% on each sale.

My Services

My salon provides:

- The following hair services: _____

- The following nail services: _____

- The following beauty services: _____

- The following body services: _____

- Packages of services that include: _____

My employees:

- Identify opportunities to up sell services to clients? _____

- Recommend services to _____ clients.

- Convert _____% into sales.

- Receive a commission of _____% on each service.

My Clients

My ideal client:

- Looks like: _____
- Shops at: _____
- Owns: _____
- Wears: _____
- Drives: _____
- Has an income of: _____
- Desires these products: _____
- Desires these services: _____
- Expects: _____

When clients come to my salon the first time, they will:

- Feel: _____
- Think: _____
- Say to themselves: _____
- Purchase: _____

When my clients leave my salon after their first visit, they will:

- Recommend us to their friends because: _____
- Return because: _____
- Buy products that will: _____
- Return to take advantages of what services? _____
- Become loyal clients because: _____

My Business

When I look at my business I:

- Say: _____

- Think: _____

- Feel: _____

- Believe: _____

My product lines and services:

- Attract my ideal client by: _____

- Are used by my clients because: _____

- Provide my clients with: _____

- Offer educational opportunities to my staff? _____

- Are not for sale in supermarkets and drug stores? _____

My business:

- Has a profit of: _____

- Has _____ employees.

- Is known for: _____

- Is a key part of the local community because: _____

Get Organized Checklist

It's time to get organized with your business. We recommend making a binder with several sections that focus on key areas in your salon. Each section is broken down into smaller, more manageable tasks. Here's a sample of how your binder might look.

And don't get intimidated as you look at this list. Some of this you may have thought of and some of it may be new, but much of it we will cover in later chapters or have covered in our other Ready, Set, Go! guides.

Tabs

1. Location
2. Business Plan
3. Incorporation/Corporate Structure
4. Financial and Accounting
5. Operational

6. Website
7. Risk Management
8. Revenue
9. Branding
10. Marketing/Advertising
11. Furniture and Equipment
12. Retail Product and Suppliers

Under each tab in your binder, you should include the following information:

Location

1. Print out maps and check out the competition in the area
2. Take pictures of the areas you are looking at
3. Research lease and/or purchase costs in the areas you desire
4. Include the contact information for leasing or real estate agents in the area
5. Find at least three suitable locations to look at

Business Plan

1. Create a business plan (you may need to enlist the help of a business coach or small business assistance group)
2. Capital investment
3. Forecasting, goals, and revenue streams
4. Executive summary

Incorporation

1. Incorporate business (or establish an LLC or other structure you and your accountant decide is best)
2. Occupational license
3. Create legal business documents
4. Buy-Sell agreements
5. Open business checking account
6. Agree on partner capital investments (if any)
7. Name registration
8. Obtain business license

9. Obtain EIN (Employment Identification Number)
10. Review all laws for the license and registration requirements

Financial and Accounting

1. Establish payment methods – credit cards, PayPal, finance options
2. Terms and conditions of payment through suppliers
3. Billing, accounts payable, inventory, POS (point of sale), scheduling, and salon software
4. Create detailed financial projections, including what it will take to reach those goals
5. Explore Small Business Administration (SBA) loans, grants, and other available governmental subsidies
6. Speak with an equipment lease financing company about other financial options

Operational

1. Assign duties and responsibilities for running aspects of the business
2. Number of employees, positions, and skills needed
3. Necessary supplies needed for budget
4. Create a relationship with your preferred shipper (UPS, FedEx, DHL)
5. Employee training/employee handbook
6. Employment agreements/contracts
7. Payroll program or a company that provides Automated Data Processing (ADP) or payroll services
8. Secure relationships with retail suppliers

Website

1. Conceptualize purpose of layout and Web presence
2. Hire Web designer
3. Hire writer
4. Create domain
5. Establish email addresses
6. Evaluate and determine the best Web resource for product sales (use eBay or Craigslist or build your own online store)
7. Evaluate the need for an online appointment booking system
8. Displays and accurately executes your mission statement

Risk Management

1. Business insurance
2. Personal disability insurance
3. Insurance on property and equipment
4. Legal agreements with suppliers
5. Legal agreements with employees
6. Umbrella insurance policy

Revenue

1. Identify revenue streams (salon services, beauty services, spa services, medical spa services, consultations, retail sales)
2. Create a catalog of merchandise
3. Establish pricing methodology for retail sales

Branding

1. Secure the services of a local branding expert if you are having trouble coming up with a name and a logo for your salon
2. Hire a graphic designer to assist with logo development (branding expert may work with a designer)
3. Develop business cards, letterhead, paper supplies, and salon menu
4. Set up phone systems with script for answering and a pleasant voicemail message

Marketing/Advertising

1. Establish social media presence through Google Places, Bing Places, Facebook, twitter, foursquare, and other social platforms
2. Develop slogans
3. Examine advertising opportunities
4. Establish advertising budget
5. Design and place ads
6. Hire a publicist to write a press release announcing your opening, or write your own press release

Furniture and Equipment

1. Salon furniture

2. Salon equipment

3. Office equipment and furniture

4. Reception area equipment and furniture

5. Retail area display cases and lighting

6. Specialty equipment (for beauty, spa, or medical spa services)

Retail Product and Suppliers

1. Establish relationships with retail suppliers

2. Develop a formula that simplifies retail product pricing

3. Note order minimums and special order incentives

4. Establish a relationship with shipping companies in your area

5. Arrange a neat, inviting retail sales area

6. Develop a script for retail sales, including points to up sell customers to another product

7. Note any seminars, classes, or talks you can attend about retail sales and the sales process

8. Develop a strategy for your employees to use when selling to customers

PART II

GETTING IT TOGETHER - SETTING UP YOUR SALON

CHAPTER 5

Start From the Beginning

"The beginning is the most important part of the work."

—Plato

A successful salon has a lot of moving parts. It's more than great cuts, colors and styles; it's the experience of being there, the services you offer, the results your clients see after a visit or after using the product you sold them. This book will help you get your salon there.

That being said, this book is for those of you who already have a salon or are in the final planning stages of a salon, but want to expand and include retail. For those of you starting from square one, our book *Ready, Set, Go! The Resource Guide for Opening, Remodeling, & Running a Successful Beauty Salon* will give you the information, resources, checklists and motivation it takes to get your salon off the ground. But no matter where you are with your salon, a brief review will ensure we're all on the same page when it comes to starting the journey to your dream of a profitable independent salon. To be a complete salon, you must successfully sell retail. Keep that in your mind as you read this chapter and the ones following and start to notice the presence of retail in the successful salons in your area.

Startup Costs

Now that you know your personal and business visions, we need to lay the groundwork to make them a reality. There are a number of factors to consider with a startup, and, while every situation will be a little different, we hope to shed light on some of the components – large and small – that you may have forgotten, glossed over or not even considered.

Finances are the largest single factor in starting a business of any kind. The biggest question is: "How much do I need?" The next question is: "Does it come from business loans, personal savings or investors?"

Costs to Consider

- Salon furniture and equipment (calculate new and used equipment)
- Spa furniture and equipment (calculate new and used equipment)
- Retail display furniture (calculate new, used, and repurposed equipment – more on this later)
- Office and backroom furnishings – tables, chairs, refrigerator, microwave, washers/dryers, desks, filing cabinets, safe, et cetera (calculate new and used equipment)
- Computer system equipment – desktop/laptop/tablet, printer, scanner, fax machine, internet expenses, POS (Point of Sale) software, accounting software and systems, inventory control systems (often integrated with accounting and POS), time logs for employees, et cetera
- Signage (internal and outdoor)
- Business Cards
- Advertising and public relations
- Phone system
- Sound system
- Lighting
- Display cases
- Reception-area furniture
- Initial retail products purchased
- Initial wholesale/salon-purposed products purchased
- Insurance
- Miscellaneous equipment – towels, cleaning supplies, break room and restroom supplies
- Televisions and other client-entertainment pieces (if needed)
- Construction costs to build a new facility or remodel an existing space
- Plus an additional 20% for unforeseen expenses and maintenance expenses (like light bulbs, plumbers, et cetera)

When Michael Haase wanted to grow the number of salons he owned, he bought one that was already operating successfully. What was his biggest mistake?

"My mistake was failing to train my team before I opened the doors, and my initial interview process was weak. I learned that at the end of the day, you must start fresh and create new, just as you would with a new client."

Other Factors

Through the rest of this section, we'll look at designing and planning your space, technology and computer systems to consider, and break down your salon by zone in order to identify other factors that will have an impact on your plan for a new or remodeled retail-focused salon.

When you are building a new salon, remodeling an existing space or doing something as simple as installing new shelves or station furniture, construction timelines are an issue. Take a look at what Fever Hair Design had to say about timelines.

"Thinking that construction would only take 30 days, simply because that's what the contractor told me, I watched it drag out to 90 days (and double in cost) while I went without income."

How do you protect yourself from this happening? Unfortunately, issues come up with construction – the cabinet is difficult to build or install, there's a problem with permitting, you need to bring in the plumber and electrician unexpectedly – but you can protect yourself a bit with good planning.

Planning Points

Think through your project and consider the following

- If you're moving walls to accommodate retail, it's far more complicated than installing shelving, allow the right amount of time for that. You never know what you'll discover once you pull down sheetrock. Issues with wiring, plumbing and support structures are often more complex than you realize.

- Who is involved? Will you need the carpenter, engineer, architect, interior designer, cabinetmaker, tile guy, plumber and electrician?

- Scheduling the work. Your contractor should be able to schedule the arrival of all the workers (and their supplies) for maximum efficiency.

- Inspection. Do you need to have the work inspected? When does the inspector make site visits? If you need to make corrections, when does he come back?

- How long will it take? Ask your contractor for a window of best- to worst-case timelines and plan appropriately.

- Always consider the longer, more expensive option when planning your finances.

- Any delays in opening mean lost revenue for you, as the salon owner, and your employees.

THE PROS KNOW

"I did plenty of research on who my competition would be. Plus I needed to be in close proximity to my customers. I built a great customer base over 10 years. I also have plenty of parking in the plaza. My customers feel safe and I have a strong anchor [store] in my plaza."

Maria Arias
Nolan Vincent Salons, Davie, FL

CHAPTER 6

Location, Location, Location

"There's a place and means for every man alive."

—William Shakespeare

We all know the saying "Location, location, location," and it's as true in retail as it is in real estate. The location of your salon affects everything from how you are perceived to your signage, the services you offer and even your pricing. Whether you're adding retail to an existing salon or starting from scratch, your location can help, or hurt, your retail sales. Do your research and decide on your location carefully, it's a factor that will play a large role in the success of your salon and the longevity of your business.

THE PROS KNOW

"The importance of your location is key to business success. I chose my location due to customer demographics, plenty of parking, because it's close to the beach and a very high-end customer base living close by."

Harrison Sasser
Gentleman's Corner, Wilmington, NC

What to Look For

Once you've done your research, it's easy to identify the places your clients frequent. Maybe it's an upscale, boutique-filled shopping center, maybe it's a city street filled with neighborhood shops, maybe it's something in between.

But it doesn't stop there. Take a look at these factors that will affect your decision.

Location Consideration

- ○ Does the location have ample parking?
- ○ Is it easy to pull in and out of the parking lot?
- ○ Is there a traffic light or stop sign that may make it easier for clients to get in and out during high-traffic days?
- ○ How much traffic drives by the location? (The Department of Transportation or city traffic department can often provide this information.)
- ○ How much traffic walks by the location? (Though you want a loyal, returning client base, don't underestimate the buying power of walk-in clients, especially for your retail sales.)
- ○ What are the shopping center's regulations on signage and exterior lighting?
- ○ Does the city have ordinances over signage?
- ○ What other businesses are nearby? (If you are looking for an upscale client, you should surround yourself with upscale stores. If you are looking for a family client base, you should find a location near other family-friendly dining and shopping destinations.)
- ○ Is the area you're considering under good repair? Are sidewalks clean and unbroken, streetlights maintained, street and parking lot surface maintained and pothole free?
- ○ How visible would your salon be from the street? From the parking lot?
- ○ Is your location easy to find?
- ○ Is the area safe at night?

Meet Your Neighbors

When you're considering a location, pay a visit to neighboring stores. If all goes well, you'll be business neighbors for years to come and their insight into the area, their products and their personalities will drive your final decision.

- Do their price points, product lines and services fall in line with what you offer?
- Are any of them competing directly with your retail or service offerings?

Having, and being, a good neighbor can benefit your business as well as neighboring businesses. Build a relationship with your neighbors and join forces (and combine money) to throw a "block party" with specials that drive customers to all the stores. Pull it off successfully and your reputation as a business, business owner and neighbor will grow.

- Are the owners and employees friendly?
- What do they have to say about their location?
- Can you share a customer base?
- Will your customers patronize nearby shops? Will theirs patronize yours?

Personal Factors

Your location shouldn't just support your business; it should also support your lifestyle.

- How long will it take you to get to and from work? Are you comfortable with that commute?
- How close is your bank?
- Is there a place for you and employees to eat lunch affordably?
- If you need to take your kids to school, where are their school and afterschool programs located in relation to your salon?

Retail Details

One thing many business owners forget to consider in their location decision is retail. Sure, most think of pricing their products and services on par with their neighbors (which salon sells more $40 shampoo, one located beside a bargain store or one beside an upscale dress shop?), but many don't think of their location in terms of product availability.

Many wholesale suppliers work in "territories" determined by zip code, geography, proximity to competitors or any of a hundred other factors, and their sales representatives only sell to a limited number of retailers in their territory. Identify the products you want to carry, contact your territory sales representative and talk to them about availability. You may find that your location is inside an exclusive territory held by a competitor, but your second choice, only a few blocks away, works.

Size Matters

Your salon is not only a place for traditional salon services – cut, color, style – but you want to sell retail and may have the desire to offer other beauty, spa or med-spa services. Does your desired location have room for all this? You'll need at least 1,200 square feet of salon space for six operators (that includes a small reception area and a small storeroom). If you want a dedicated retail area, add another 500-800 square feet, plus another 400 for product storage. If you desire a spacious reception area, add another 400 square feet. If you're adding other beauty or spa services, you'll need even more room.

We'll cover size and design in a later chapter, but you can see that it is a major consideration when selecting your location.

Check off the questions below as you find out the answers.

- ◯ Is my location zoned for a salon with retail?
- ◯ Is it large enough for my business?
- ◯ Does it match my desired layout?
- ◯ What repairs or remodeling efforts are needed?
- ◯ Is the location convenient to your life (home, school, et cetera)?
- ◯ Is the location convenient for employees (affordable lunch, shopping, et cetera)?
- ◯ Does the location cater to your desired client?
- ◯ Does the location (and area) have the image you are looking for?
- ◯ Is it a safe neighborhood?
- ◯ Are neighboring businesses complimentary to your salon?
- ◯ Will they attract clients to your salon?
- ◯ Will your salon attract clients for their stores?
- ◯ Are there many competitors nearby?
- ◯ Are you within the territory to sell the products you desire?
- ◯ Can delivery and service trucks easily access your location?
- ◯ Is parking adequate?
- ◯ Can you see the location from the street?
- ◯ Will your location attract walk-in customers?
- ◯ Are exterior signs permitted?
- ◯ Are the lease or purchase terms favorable?

THE PROS KNOW

"Location is key. We are in a rival's area but we have the best location. We are one mile from the University of Connecticut campus. Parking is great and we have a young, hip clientele."

Marybeth Fiore
Hair Trendz, Storrs, CT

CHAPTER 7

How to Avoid Pitfalls in a Commercial Lease

Fact: Leases are landlord favored. They're written by the landlord. This means that every provision listed on your lease will be in their favor.

After Location, location, location, no decision a salon owner makes has more impact on her financials than when she signs a commercial lease. Some long-term leases can be for hundreds of thousands of dollars. A salon's profit leaves no room for mistakes on a commercial lease. Also understand that the commercial lease is written 100% in favor of the Landlord or "lessor."

Hire a lawyer who specializes in lease agreements. Leases can be a minefield of problems. Do not cross this treacherous territory without an experienced guide. As you make more recommendations on the lease, it will have more impact if those changes are on an attorney's letterhead.

Many salons only look at the base rent. The Common Area Maintenance "CAM" charges can be almost as much as the rent charges. Unlike your base rent which is a negotiated rate. CAM charges, without a cap, can rise as much as the landlord wants.

Do not underestimate the value of your clientele to a center. The average stylist in your salon does 50 customers a week x 50 weeks. For a 10-operator salon that is 25,000 client visits a year with an average income well above national averages. Your salon traffic can make all businesses in that center successful.

Leases are very complicated legal documents. I would ask your landlord or leasing agent for a one page summary lease of key details. I always measure the space myself. I always take pictures of the space before you take possession. Put the lease, all notes and letters in a file folder or notebook for when you have an issue.

So how do you negotiate a lease?

I suggest asking for 20 changes in the lease, knowing you may only get 10 of the changes. The key things to negotiate are the following:

1. **Personal Guarantee** – The landlord will want you to guarantee the lease with a personal guarantee. Always try to sign the lease as the salon corporation. You will probably lose this argument, but hold out to the last to use this chip to get something else. Okay….I will sign the guarantee, but I want a cap on CAM charges.

2. **Security Deposit** – Based on your financials or Personal Guarantee ask for the security deposit to be waived. They will probably say no…but it becomes a bargaining chip for later. Please add a clause that says that if the center sells the security deposit is transferred to the new owner.

3. **Repairs / Air Conditioning Repairs** – Most leases say that the leasee is responsible for all interior repairs. This is negotiable. Salon odors and hair sprays are very hard on HVAC units. They will not last 5-7 years. If you are in a long-term lease, this repair can run $5,000-$10,000, depending on the size of the unit and if it must be replaced. Ouch! I always negotiate that the first $500 of any repair will be paid by the lessee. The balance will be paid for by the landlord. If they say "No," offer the first $750, then $1,000, then $2,000. Anything you get will limit your liability in the future. (Don't forget the Personal Guarantee and Security Deposit bargaining chips).

4. **Cap on CAM** – As I mentioned earlier, CAM charges can be very costly and have no cap the owner must follow. Please cap the CAM charges...Change to 5%, 7%, and 10% annually.

5. **Escape Clause** – If you are paying premium rent on a high traffic shopping center, what happens if occupancy falls dramatically? I would negotiate an escape clause that allows you to renegotiate the rental rate if occupancy of the center falls below 50%.

6. **Gross Leasable vs. Leased space** – Always negotiate that your % of the CAM charges is based on the leasable space in the center not what is leased (What if you are the only tenant in a center? 100% CAM).

7. **Option Years** – Options are the renewal of your lease for another period of time. Options do not cost you anything unless you exercise your option to renew. ALWAYS negotiate 3-5 options at a predetermined price. You may be renting in a center that becomes very popular in the future. A lease that says you are able to exercise an option at "Market Rate" is not smart. All rates are negotiable. I would offer X$ for the first 3 years and XX$ for the next 3 years and XXX$ for the next 3 years. At some time in the future you may want to sell. Having the rent pre-negotiated at a great rate is a huge selling tool. Last but not least, I always ask for one month free rent anytime you exercise an option to redecorate your space.

8. **Parking** – Always a problem. Landlords never like to reserve spots for your business. However, what if you are near a busy restaurant and for 2 hours a day your customers cannot get close to your business? Your staff is predominately female and work late at night. I would suggest a pre determined well-lit area for your staff to park in.

THE PROS KNOW

"I hired a lease negotiator. They did everything. They earn their fee based on what they save you on your lease. Their team was amazing. I'm an expert at retail, but they are specialists in lease agreements and they've saved me thousands over the course of my lease."

Harrison Sasser
Gentlemen's Corner, Wilmington, NC

9. **Exclusive Salon in the Center** – It doesn't hurt to throw this request into your 20 negotiating points.

10. **Signage** – Most people negotiate their lease and then worry about the sign. The sign may or may not comply with your lease. Always have your sign company give you a drawing of all signage and ask that it become an addendum in the lease.

11. **Percentage Lease** – Never sign a lease with a percentage of sales clause. It is done for retail businesses, not salons. Please cross off all references to a percentage rent.

12. **Hours of Operation** – Some centers require you to be open during center hours. Please look at these hours before you sign (9 a.m.-10 p.m. is a long day).

13. **Merchants Association** - I try to eliminate from the lease. Merchants associations are expensive and it is not a great way for you to get new customers.

14. **Insurance** – Always have your insurance in affect before you do anything in the space. What if someone gets injured before you open for business?

15. **Right to Cure Clause** – In the lease you will sign, their will be multiple lessee defaults that would let your landlord move you out of the center. I always add a 10-day "Right to Cure" clause to correct any defaults. Also add to the lease that any defaults must be sent to you by registered mail.

16. **Subletting or assigning your lease** – The lease should read you can sublet or assign under reasonable conditions to a tenant of equal or better creditworthiness.

17. **Holding Over Clause** – Most leases say that if your lease has expired, you can rent month to month at 2 times your last rate. Always add to your lease the ability to rent month to month for 90 days at the last months rate. If you are moving and there is a construction delay, it could be an expensive 90 days.

How CAM Charges Can Put You Out of Business

- If you're in a strip mall that has lost tenants, your CAM charges will spike for any repairs because there are fewer parties paying into the pool.

- If you rent an old, tired mall space, expect your CAM to rise as landlords make repairs and upgrades.

- A bad snow season can raise your CAM charges to pay for snow removal.

- Tenants pay CAM on fancy landlord digs and management fees.

- When owning a salon, watch your CAM charge go through the roof due to the volume of water you use.

CHAPTER 8

Designing Your Space for Retail

"Everything is designed. Few things are designed well."

—Brian Reed

What's the atmosphere you want to create in your salon? No matter if you're looking for an exclusive, chic, relaxing or ultra-trendy (or anything else for that matter) experience, good design and decoration, a friendly floor plan and thoughtful planning for each of your zones will create the salon of your dreams.

Salons are broken down into eight zones:

- Entry
- Reception
- Retail
- Styling Floor
- Shampoo Area
- Services (manicure/pedicure/makeup consultation)
- Spa
- Restrooms, Changing Areas and Dispensory

We'll consider each in more detail, give you tips on how to design each one effectively and how to take advantage of retail sale and service sale opportunities in each, but first, let's take a look at a few salon floor plans.

From the flow of traffic from area to area to the space planning for styling and service stations (you don't want too much space or the salon looks empty, too little space and it looks cramped) to the placement of furniture and fixtures (you don't want to make a maze of chairs, retail display and the reception counter), there are a lot of elements that make a great salon.

Many salon owners will establish their business in an existing space, which means making your plans fit your place. Fortunately, many storefronts (whether on city streets, strip malls or boutique shopping villages) have the basics: sales floor, checkout/reception counter, storage, a restroom and an employee area of some sort. Often, these spaces are rectangular, which allows for quite a lot of opportunities to cost-effectively make the space into your own salon, transforming it from a basic cut and color salon to a fully functioning retail salon.

THAT'S WHAT THEY SAY

Rita Hazan of Rita Hazan Salon said that for a recent salon, she "took an empty, 8,000 square foot space and built it out exactly the way I wanted. Each outlet, each station, the floors – and this time, every single aspect was considered based on wear and tear and chosen to look beautiful and glamorous…and to last."

Take a look at these floor plans, all based on rectangular storefronts, and see how salons of various sizes can make use of a typical space.

A Cut Above Salon

750 Sq. Feet

(4) Operator Salon

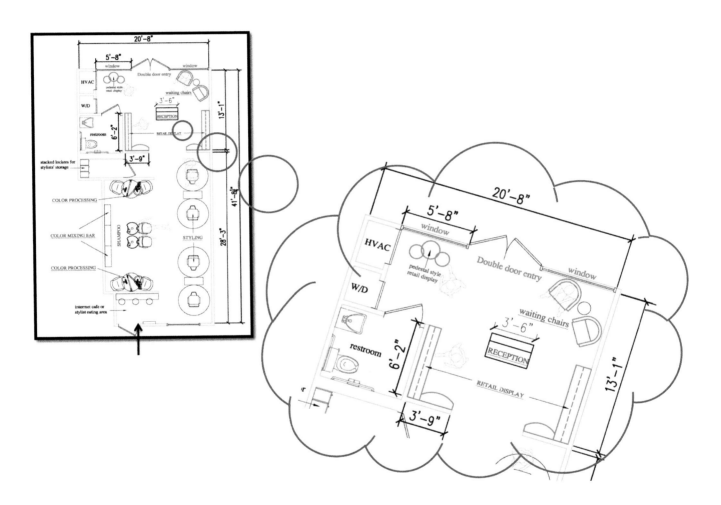

The overall salon space has been distinctly divided between a specifically designed retail area and the styling floor itself. The two large windows up front allow for a great visual into the retail section of the salon. This retail layout has been designed to mimic an actual store to attract more foot traffic and potential product sales.

Hair Color Studio

1200 Sq. Feet

(6) Operator Salon

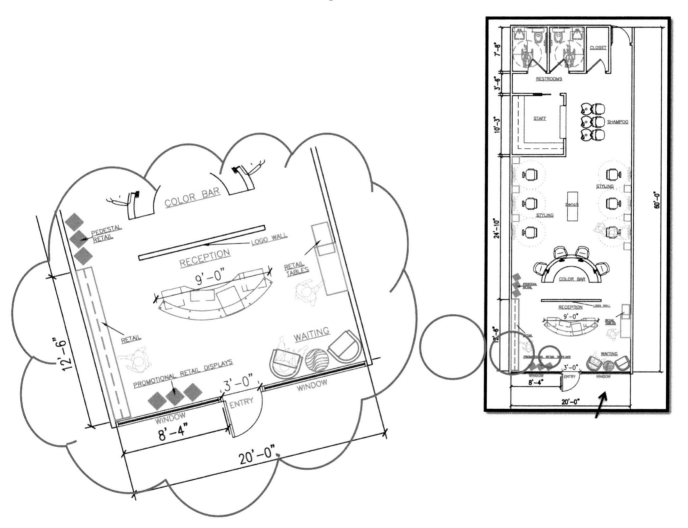

For this (6) operator salon, minimal waiting chairs were placed in the reception/retail area to encourge guests to interact with the various retail displays. The retail itself partially extends into the salon area to fill unused wall space. Plus, this slight extension allows the customers receiving salon services to maintain a visual of retail products at all times.

The Hair House

1200 Sq. Feet

(8) Operator Salon

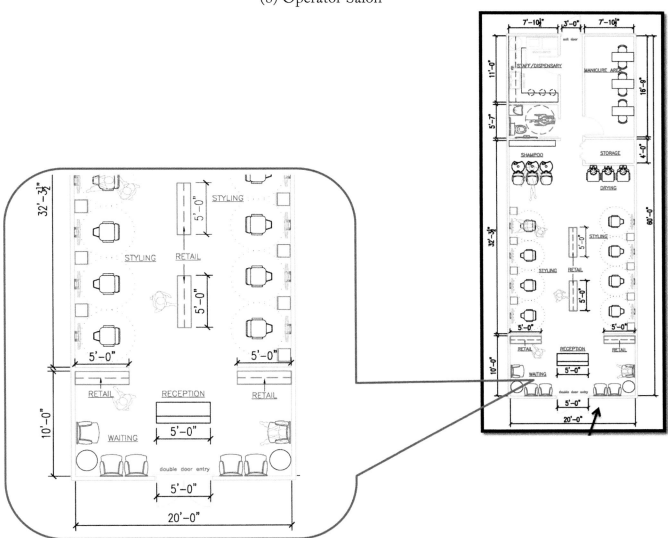

The walls behind the retail units in the front were existing when this space was designed. Due to only having 10' of depth for the reception area, additional retail diplays were placed directly on the cutting floor. Although there is a distinct separation between the reception and styling area, there is still a visual from the front leading to that extra retail. Having the retail units right in the syling area also allows the sylists to promote the products being used on their customer during a service.

— PART III —

PROFIT EVERYWHERE YOU LOOK

CHAPTER 9

Retail: What's Right for You?

"When it comes to selling, involvement, education and relevancy, of course, are as important as ever, but in the advertising din of today, unless you make yourself noticed and believed, you ain't got nothing!"

—Leo Burnett

By now, you know there is opportunity for retail sales in every part of your salon. Now it's time to start thinking of they types of retail you'll carry. This means the products, tools, and they ways they're sold.

Products and Tools

The first rule is this: if you or your employees wouldn't use it, why would you sell it? It's hard to sell a product you don't believe in, so sell what you use and use what you sell. By being a user as well as a sales person, you'll be able to speak honestly about the product and your experiences with it. Plus, as an authority on the product, your clients will look to you for guidance and if you say, "We carry product A but I always use product B," they're going to look for product B.

Selecting your products is more than just going with what you use, many other factors come into play.

Factors when Considering a Product or Service for Your Salon

- **Cost**

  What's the price of the product? Is it in line with your salon and neighboring stores? Too high and you drive customers away; too low and you appear undervalued.

- **Desire**

  Are the products ones your clients desire? Do they appeal to the ethnic, cultural and economic sensibilities of your clients?

- **Expense**

  Are the products expensive to stock? Is there a large minimum order? Will they be expensive to keep?

- **Availability**

  Are you able to carry the product (not blocked by an exclusivity area)? Can you receive the exclusive right to carry the product in your area?

- **Rules**

  Some suppliers dictate how you price and discount their items. Are there limitations on how flexible you can be regarding price, bundles, discounts and sales?

- **Display**

  Do you have the room for them? Does the supplier require certain displays or display types for their product lines?

- **Storage**

  Do you have room for storage of unused products?

- **Lifespan**

  Does the product have a limited shelf life (which increases the speed at which you need to sell)?

- **Buyback**

  Some suppliers will buy back any unused stock (sometimes at full wholesale price, sometimes at a prorated amount). Does your supplier have a similar deal?

The same thoughts apply to tools, but with an additional reminder: before your employees use a tool on a client or try to sell a tool, ensure they are properly trained on the equipment. Most of the time, it only takes a few minutes to get someone up to speed on a new tool, and it avoids situations where an employee sells a product based on a feature it doesn't have and the client returns it.

The Kinds of Retail Sales

There are a lot ways to sell your retail items, but they fall into two major categories: direct and indirect sales.

Direct Sales

This is what you typically think of with sales. It's a hands-on, active, involved process. Sometimes it's high pressure, sometimes it's not, but it's always a direct and obvious sales approach.

Examples of direct sales include asking a client what additional products they'd like, then recommending a product for them; and encouraging a client to try another product complimentary to their treatment or purchase.

Indirect Sales

This is a much lower-pressure sales approach. With indirect sales, you're more subtle and smooth. You're making sales through conversation that keeps coming back to the features and benefits of the product or tool. Indirect sales also includes product exposure (in your reception/retail area) and product use (in the styling chair).

Examples of indirect sales include listening to a client as they talk about their hair (or skin, makeup, et cetera) and recommending, casually, a product carried in the salon; talking up a product as you use it on them; or a stunning and inviting retail display in front of them while they wait.

Impulse Buys

Don't forget the impulse sales. What are impulse sales? They're small items (with a big markup) that clients will pick up and purchase with little thought or consideration.

Think of the grocery store. In the checkout line you're surrounded by batteries, magazines, drinks, snacks, eyeglass repair kits, sample and travel size items, cards, lighters, toothpicks, matches and 1,000 other things. How many times have you picked up a magazine, then a drink and maybe some gum, only to find you just spent an additional $10? We know we're guilty of doing that, but we also recognize how smart stores are for surrounding their customers with easy opportunities to buy when they are so close to the end of their shopping experience. Do the same in your salon.

THAT'S WHAT THEY SAY

When it comes to retail, what does Van Council of Van Michael Salons in Atlanta, GA., believe?

"One of the biggest mistakes I made initially as a salon owner was having too many product lines. It overcomplicated the product pitch, and in the end we missed sales, which lowered profitability. When we partnered exclusively with one manufacturer, I was able to offer focused service and products. As my salons needed renovations or as we opened new locations, we started positioning retail at the front of the salon, thereby creating a 'retail store.' This welcomed walk-ins and created opportunities to gain new guests."

THE PROS KNOW

"We sell using all the senses – the music, the smells, the way things feel, it's all designed to entice the guest into buying."

Jill Krahn
Hair Success Salons and Spas, Fargo, ND

CHAPTER 10

In the Zone: The Doorway to Wealth

Why Your Entrance is Important

"An entry is like a great party invitation: it sets the tone for what's to come."

—Tobi Fairley

First impressions are everything and the exterior of your salon is your first chance to make an impression on clients and potential (walk-in or drive-by) clients. Our experience in the industry has given us some special insight into creating an inviting front entrance to your salon.

Doorway to Wealth

The front entrance of your business is the first impression your customers new or old establish the minute they walk through those doors. You do not get a second chance to make a first impression. An untidy, drab or obscure storefront puts off customers, even sends foot traffic away. Just a few simple things can draw new customers, close sales and boost your bottom line.

The front entrance plays a special role in the energy that flows through your place of business. The front door should be considered your location of opportunity. Every time a customer walks through those doors, another opportunity arises. We all know that opportunities bring greater wealth, new customers, happier employees and increased salaries, which makes for a healthy profitable business.

THE PROS KNOW

"Your doorway and entrance, they have to appeal to all five of your senses. You have one shot and that's it; make it a good one."

Jill Krahn
Hair Success Salon and Spas, Fargo, ND

Create an identity – Since the entrance is the first clue a customer has of what lies beyond the door, it is important to create a clear defined identity, you can do this by using items that hint the personality and uniqueness of what your business has to offer. It can be a distinctive welcome plaque, the symbol of the retail brands you are selling hanging on your door or wall as you enter, a unique picture, fixture or items that represent you and your staff; be creative!

Supportive entryway – Use hip height items around the entryway to offer stable energetic support. Why? Because hip high energy represent "cane" energy, what people use when they are unsteady on their feet to support them as they move outside to in. Items and furnishings, rails, walls at hip height promote and offer a subtle sense of safety. Entranceways that have the feeling of support are less stressful to cross and encourage shoppers to relax and not feel uncomfortable. Large bare entranceways scare people and often intimidate the first time customer. This immediately turns of their buying senses creating negative energy and a sense of trepidation towards services or retail they may have wanted before entering your place of business.

Establishing a sense of safety – How many times have we looked up an address for a restaurant or place of business on line and had no idea where you were going or what the storefront looked like. As you get closer to the location your senses arise and you feel your body getting excited as the anticipation grows knowing you will soon be at your destination.

How do you feel when you finally get there at the entrance is dimly lit, cluttered with debris and garbage and the front window and door are not clean. You can barely see inside and immediately think what did you get yourself into and why in the world did you come. You immediately want to drive away and turn around and go home. When a customer does not feel safe entering a place of business you can forget about gaining new customers or keeping the ones you have. Your front door should always be clean, well lit and in view of everyone to see.

Simple changes to invite your customers – If you follow these concepts when creating your entrance, you are not only establishing a sense of safety and connectivity for those who walk up to your place of business, you are issuing an invitation for those customers to enter. Imagine yourself in the shoes of a first time customer when you look at the entrance of your business. What do you see? How do you feel? Do you see a place that is inviting? Do you understand what type of business you are stepping into? Do you feel excited about entering this doorway? Do you feel like you can't wait to get in or do you want to turn and run away?

Following the suggestions below will enable you do establish the "cant wait to get into your business mentality!"

Step 1

Clean the storefront daily. Remove clutter, dust and dirt top to bottom. Clean the door handle and make sure if you have a glass door it is cleaned before you open for business. Just by sweeping the sidewalks and cleaning the door and windows daily, you demonstrate the pride you take in your business and over time, this leads to consumer confidence.

Step 2

Hang a storefront banner. Make the most of your entrance by promoting your brand the retail that your store sells. Your sign, window displays should not overwhelm your clients, but should be easy to read. Place the banner in the window display, over your entry door or hung on the exterior façade to attract new business.

Step 3

Place a welcome mat in front of your entry door. This mat symbolizes that the owner is welcoming you into his place of business. What a wonderful felling your customers will have when they step into your business. Make sure you change the mat as soon as you see it gets worn and replace it with a new one.

Step 4

Install an awning, which gives a sense of security. People are much more likely to stop and look at the window and peek inside and enter a store that was kind enough to protect them from the elements. This business philosophy allows retail business owners the ability to display their merchandise outside to draw customers regardless of the weather.

Don't overdo it – When you own a retail store, your front door are the first chance you have to make an impression on your customers. You must remember that however you decide to establish this first impression it is very easy to overdo it and instead of drawing shoppers in you can drive them away. Keep in mind that sometimes less is more.

THE PROS KNOW

"You must hit the retail area first. Our guests love the fact that they walk into a store then a salon. My outside is brick with beautiful awnings painted black with white trim. We have many walk-in customers because of the cool, slick vibe the building gives off."

Marybeth Fiore
Hair Trendz, Storrs, CT

Did you follow these steps to make your store front inviting?

- Less is more when it comes to your front door and window displays. A cluttered front door and window is an instant turnoff to customers.

- Make your merchandise your focal point.

- Make sure your front door is well lit and your customers feel safe when entering.

- Place a welcome mat in front of your door

- Clean your front door and entrance handle at the start of each day

- Make sure your doorway is clean.

- Make your windows tell your story. They should sell beauty, hair, the services your clients want and the lifestyles they want to lead.

- Display featured products in the window (more on this later).

- Use tasteful signage with clear, legible lettering (no script ever, it's hard to read).

- Use contrasting colors and textures to create interest.

- Have your name out front. Naming your salon is a tricky thing and we'll cover that in a later chapter, but to be noticed and to be easily found, your name has to appear prominently somewhere outside your salon, both on the street (if your town allows street signage or your shopping center has a store directory) and over the door (or in the window).

CHAPTER 11

In the Zone: Retail Success

"Buying is a profound pleasure."

—Simone de Beauvoir

Far too many salons overlook one of the easiest avenues for increased revenue – retail. Retail sales can help put a salon on solid financial footing, bring in increased profits for both owners and employees, and even help make a name for the salon in the community. How? We'll go into the specifics in just a few chapters, for now, let's look at the shape, size and structure of a salon retail zone.

The First Thing You See...

Many salon designers will tell you that every salon needs dedicated retail space in their reception area. They're right. The reception area is a place where clients congregate before seeing stylists and a place they pause while completing payment and scheduling their next appointment, so it only makes sense for retail and reception to blend into one another or even occupy the same space. (Opportunities exist for passive and active selling at both times and we'll get into more detail on taking advantage of those opportunities later.) But that's not the only place where retail fits in with your floor plan.

Fact

The majority of haircare products are purchased outside the salon.

Have you considered the following areas?

- Signage and product displays often provided by suppliers
- Windows
- The styling floor
- The stylist's chair
- The styling session
- Shampoo and color stations

THAT'S WHAT THEY SAY

Ted Gibson of ted gibson salons embraced retail, and the impact it's had on his business is staggering.

"[I] can only do so many haircuts and colors in a day, but selling retail enables [me] to offer benefits, amenities and extras in the salon. I didn't take that into account when I opened my first salon, but since then I have made drastic changes. We focus on retail and have built a business that grew 45% in the past year."

How Much Space?

Dealing with how much space is devoted to retail can be difficult. Depending on the layout of your store, whether you own, rent, or are building new, and a dozen other factors, you may have more or less space to devote to retail. But let's be clear on one thing: a successful salon must integrate retail sales into their strategy in order to maximize profit opportunities and provide clients with a one-stop-shop for their beauty needs.

When clients walk into your salon, if they enter a professional hair care and beauty product shop that also performs salon treatments, they are more likely to walk out with the products you sold them. We recommend that at least five feet of wall space to either side of the reception desk be dedicated to retail display, as well as the area behind the reception desk. In addition, tables, pedestals and window displays should be interspersed in the area.

So, how much space are we talking about? For a salon with up to 10 stations, we recommend 200-300 square feet. That amount of square footage creates a cozy, but not cramped feel when you include 4-6 waiting chairs, the reception counter and retail space.

For larger salons, or for those interested in becoming the authority on the products that support their services, more space may be necessary, but not more than say 500 contiguous square feet of dedicated retail (at that size it begins to feel overwhelming).

When considering retail opportunities in other zones throughout the salon, the square footage depends largely on your layout and traffic flow, although we would recommend using tables, open or two-sided shelving units and the like as dividers between sections of the salon. This keeps the styling floor separate from the shampoo area while functioning as a retail center. Space for these outlying retail zones can run from one to 20 square feet, and can take the shape of everything from floating wall shelves to manufacturer-provided floor displays.

What Do I Use?

The beauty of owning your own salon is that you determine the tone the décor establishes, and that means that when it comes to retail display, the sky's the limit. While cost may be a concern when it comes to selecting your retail display units, keep in mind two things: one, your retail area will be a money-making center for the salon; and, two, you can find chic displays on any budget.

Depending on the style of your salon, you'll be looking in different places for retail display units. We have a list of some places where you can look and the types of things you can expect to find there; use the list as a starting point in your search for display units, but remember to keep it fun, keep it creative, keep an open mind and keep an eye out for ways to repurpose or re-present unusual pieces for your purpose.

- **Antique Stores.** Perfect for finding antique apothecary cases, freestanding bookshelves, chifforobes, medicine cabinets, medical and retail display units and other furniture and décor items.

- **Restaurant Supply Store.** Restaurant supply stores carry a variety of furniture pieces designed for professional kitchen and pantry storage, but, depending on your salon's look, this industrial, wire framed shelving; and metal and wood-topped butcher blocks and tables could be just the piece you're looking for. Don't overlook the potential in pot racks and overhead storage systems.

- **Local Craftsmen.** For a custom look or size, enlist the services of a local craftsman. These cabinetmakers and furniture makers can often produce and install shelving units quickly and cost effectively.

- **Ikea.** Many urban areas have an Ikea – the Swedish furniture and home goods giant – nearby. Ikea is perfect for low-cost, easy to assemble retail display options. From their standard bookcases to their custom retail solutions and specialized storage, display and decoration pieces that fit almost any store, Ikea's furniture, and their planners, will help you get started.

- **Hardware Stores.** If Ikea is do-it-yourself-lite, then hardware stores are the full-bodied version. At a hardware store you can get anything from materials to build your own cabinet to stock kitchen cabinets and storage shelving, to brackets and boards to build you own shelves. Prices vary by unit or board foot (for shelving).

Types of Units

Retail display units come in all shapes and sizes but are broken down into two general categories: wall and floor units. We'll get into the placement of these in more detail later, but for now, think about how a combination of the right wall and floor units can work for your salon

Wall Units

Wall units come in any number of sizes and shapes. From standard retail shelving to floating shelves to glass shelves to specialized units designed to display specific products, they all have one thing in common: they are attached to or sit against the wall.

Many times, wall units you get from a supplier will have lightboxes or display windows built in, or will incorporate a product line's name or company logo on the unit. These kinds of units often look very sleek, chic and cutting edge and may not go with your salon's vibe.

Wall units are available from almost anywhere, from a local craftsman to Ikea to an antique store or vintage shop. What you get and how you put it together depends on the salon experience you're creating.

Floor Units

Floor units, called freestanding units by some, are any arrangement of shelves, tables or displays designed to stand on the floor without being anchored to a wall. These include tables, pedestals, square, rectangular and tower displays that allow clients to view products from any side. Pedestals come in all shapes and sizes (tall to short, small to large, slim to bulky) and we recommend using a variety of pedestals to add interest to your retail.

> **NOTE**
>
> Having a hard time picturing the layout of your retail area or other part of your salon? Head over to the nearest liquor store. No, not for a drink, for boxes.
>
> Try to get boxes around the same size and then build your "retail units" in place where you think they'll go. Simply stack the boxes on top of one another and approximate the shape and size of the furniture, displays and other obstacles you're having a tough time visualizing. Sure, your salon may look like a storage area for a day or two, but with the box exercise, you can eliminate a lot of regret down the road.
>
> Liquor stores and large mega-marts have plenty of boxes to go around, stop by and pick some up. Depending on the size of your space, you may need two or more loads of boxes.

Bring your style into the salon – it should look and feel they way you want and reveal your personality at the same time – but remember to leave room for the personalities and styles of your employees and clients. You don't want to over stylize or over decorate the salon, you want it to be tasteful, no matter the style. Restraint is the key between overdone décor and creating an effective atmosphere.

THE PROS KNOW

"Owners tend to over-develop the styling area. They don't realize the importance of the design of their retail area. You're either in retail or you're not. If you're not, you're not in the game of beauty."

David Osgood
R.G. Shakoun Salons, Nashua, NH

"The retail area has to be designed with easy access to exit the salon. Buying on the way out the door is a must. I make the guest walk through a maze of retail to reach the checkout counter."

Jill Krahn
Hair Success Salon and Spas, Fargo, ND

CHAPTER 12

In the Zone: Styling Floor and Salon Services

"Luxury must be comfortable, otherwise it is not luxury."

—Coco Chanel

As we mentioned in the previous chapter, there are retail opportunities throughout your salon. Sure, they may take up a little floor space, but if you sell the right products in the right ways, the money in the cash register will overshadow the few square feet you lose with displays. Many salon owners tend to put in extra styling stations with the hope of someday having stylists to fill those chairs, neglecting and cutting back on the necessary and profitable retail area. Years later, they have a lot of lost revenue from retail sales and the chairs sit empty.

The Styling Floor:

You've already exposed your clients to your product lines in the reception area and now it's time to take them in for their service and that means it's time for another exposure to the product.

The path from reception to your stylists' chairs shouldn't be a straight line. It seems illogical, but it makes selling sense. Lead them through or around at least one more retail zone before they reach the chair. The products here can be different – a higher-end line, salon-quality products or tools – or the same as in reception, the point here is exposure and repetition. The more a consumer is exposed to a product, the more likely they are to purchase it. That's why we want to show them the products early and often.

This secondary retail zone doesn't have to be a large wall unit or an imposing floor system; it can be a trio of pedestals with only two or three products on each, or a table and rack of small items like makeup and brushes or other tools. Again, the idea is exposure and repetition, so show your clients the products you want them to buy or use.

Tips

Selling retail becomes easier when you sell to the five senses: sight, sound, touch, taste and smell.

The Styling Chair

What are your clients doing while they're in the styling chair? We know, they do the same things we do: chat with the stylists, thumb through a magazine or styling lookbook, and look around the salon. Why not give them something to look at? Why not give them one more exposure to the products – shampoo, styling clay (or gel or paste or wax), brushes, personal trimmers, whatever – the stylists will use on them?

Imagine if on the wall between each station you had three glass shelves (much like the glass shelves Pottery Barn and similar stores carry for bathrooms) arranged with only a handful of products. These products are the ones the stylist will reach for and use throughout the service. In doing so, you accomplish three things (in addition to that extra exposure):

1. The client sees the product in action

2. The client experiences the product

3. The stylist has the chance to sell them on the benefits, features and advantages of the product

Or imagine if you used a simple shelving unit accessible from both sides (like Ikea's Expedit shelves) to give each station some privacy and display selected retail products. Again, you have exposure, you have an opportunity for the clients to see and experience the product (and maybe even try it themselves) and you give the stylist a chance to sell the product.

As you can see, there are a lot of easy, non-obtrusive opportunities to sell on your salon's styling floor. In a few chapters, we'll get into some specifics about systems, products, prices and sourcing for retail display in every zone.

✓ CHECK IT OUT

How Does Your Salon Engage Your Clients With Retail?

- Product displays at every styling station encourages clients to ask questions and encourages stylists to utilize the product they're selling. How much area have you devoted to retail at each styling station?

- First impressions are everything. When clients walk into your salon, are they immediately engaged by retail products?

- While clients are waiting for their stylist, they can play on their phones, read a magazine or check out interesting retail displays. What parts of your retail display are visible and accessible by clients who are waiting to be seen?

- There are a number of opportunities to sell retail products to your clients. Your stylists are selling at their chairs, your displays are selling in the waiting area, but are you selling at the reception desk? It's the perfect place to engage customers when they come it and while they wait to pay. How effective is your reception desk when it comes to retail sales?

CHAPTER 13

In the Zone: Golden Opportunities – Spa and Services, Restrooms and Dressing Areas

"A wise man will make more opportunities than he finds."

—Francis Bacon

As with your styling floor and stylists' chairs, you have an opportunity to sell when your clients are waiting on their services or spa treatments to be completed. From the shampoo area to the coloring stations to manicure, pedicure and other spa treatment stations to massage rooms, you have the chance to display products, let clients experience them and deliver a winning (but not too pushy) sales pitch.

Passive Attention

When your clients are in the chair, foil in their hair, waiting for the color to set, what do they do? Probably the same thing they do in the styling chair: play on their phone, read a magazine and talk to their stylist or another client. They're passive, rooted to one place and looking for something to do while they wait. So, like when they're in the styling chair, give them something else to look at, read or view. How would the following strategies impact your salon's retail sales?

> **Fact**
>
> You have less than 15 seconds to make a first impression on a customer and make an impact that will influence a retail sale, after that, it's much harder to convince them to buy.

- Having a neatly organized selection of the shampoo and conditioners the clients will use? These, of course, are for sale, and the stylist or shampooist will be sure to let the clients know that.

- Selling color kits that allow clients to pre-buy coloring treatments at a fixed price.

- Installing big, bright, poppy display ads (posters, signs and the like) showing off the colors available at the coloring station.

- Arranging a display of the tools, polishes and products for at-home manicure or pedicure touch ups and nail treatments, then having your nail technicians give a few pointers on doing it yourself for emergency fixes between appointments.

- Putting together stations where clients can try out facial wash, scrubs, tools, makeup, moisturizer and the like?

These are only a few of the opportunities for sales and product exposure that exist within your salon. By using these, and other strategies (some of which we'll bring up later, some of which you'll discover on your own), can you increase retail sales – and therefore retail profit – by 10%, 20% or even 30%? Then what are you waiting on?

Smooth Sales

Spa treatments and therapies, facials, makeup sessions, manicures, pedicures and other treatments your salon may offer provide you with more opportunities to sell, and not just passively. With a smooth sales approach, your stylists, therapists, nail techs and other employees can sell clients on products and tools in a subtle, natural manner. Why is this important? Besides increasing sales and revenue, it establishes your employees as authorities in the clients' eyes. Being an expert means being trusted, and being trusted means people listen to your recommendations.

> **Fact**
>
> Did you know that 70% of all salon customers are never offered a recommendation on a retail product? More shockingly, 50% said they would buy if their stylist would just recommend the right products for them.

Imagine if your employees would find sales opportunities like this:

- During a color or highlight: explain in detail how using a color-protection shampoo and conditioner will assist in holding color longer. If your customer pays top dollar for a color treatment, they'll be happy to pay top dollar for something that will make that color last longer.

- During the final minutes of a hair service: no matter if it's a cut, color, blowout or simple styling, mention a volumizing root booster and demonstrate it on them.• During a nail treatment: talking up the importance of quality tools (files, clippers, cuticle cutters, trimmers) and products (moisturizers, polish removers, nail strengtheners, polishes).

- During a facial: explaining how a tool (like the ClairSonic Mia) can help the client keep their skin looking healthy and clear between treatments.

- During a facial: taking the time to talk about the value of the high-quality scrubs, cleansers and moisturizers the esthetician is using.

- During a makeup session: pointing out the benefits of the line you carry, and demonstrating techniques for makeup application, giving clients some information on how to properly apply their makeup at home (which will, in turn, make them want to use your products).

- During the salon treatment (think cut and style): showing clients how to use tools and products to style their own hair.

What other opportunities exist in your salon?

You might not think about these last two areas as places with opportunity for retail sales, but don't forget the restrooms and dressing areas in your salon. We know, you're wondering how you sell – and what you sell – in the restroom. Trust us. The answer is simpler than you think.

Shampoo Area

Many salons lose focus on how important this area can be. It's usually the first part of the service of getting a cut or color and is a great place to sell some products. The shampoo and conditioner you're using should be on display and your stylists, colorists or shampooists should talk up the products and deliver a sales pitch to clients.

If during the experience of getting a wonderful scalp massage and shampoo, the client hears about how this particular product can help them have healthier hair or skin, and they enjoy the shampoo, they'll be more likely to buy.

Your shampoo area can also be a profit center in your salon simply by adding special hair treatments (Keratin treatments, Morrocan Oil treatments, et cetera) and by selling the products.

Restrooms

It may seem in bad taste to discuss what products we use in the restroom, but let's do it.

What products do you use in the restroom?

- Toilet tissue (let's get that one out of the way)
- Soap
- Towels
- Moisturizer
- Makeup (nothing wrong with freshening up while you're alone with a mirror)
- Air freshener (candle, oil diffuser, essential oils, spray, et cetera)

What retail opportunities exist here? Once you knock toilet tissue off the list (we're assuming your clients can pick this up on their own), there's plenty.

Soap:

From handmade soap bars made by local artisans to fine imported soap from France (or the country of your choosing) to custom aromatherapy blended liquid soap, everyone uses it and if they like it, they'll want to buy it. Why not give it to them? Your artisans, importers, and aromatherapy blenders wouldn't mind selling you more and getting their product in the hands of more users. It's a good idea for several reasons: you give clients something they can experience and buy, and your profit margin (the difference between purchase and sale price) is generally large on items like this.

Towels:

You might not think it, but the towels you use in your restroom say a lot about your salon. Do you use the scratchy, industrial, brown paper towels? Or do you use a better, softer paper towel? Or do you use hand towels or small linen (or terry cloth) towels? Are they branded (do they have your logo and name on them)? (most importantly) Are they available for purchase?

Not everyone will buy a hand towel, but you'd be surprised at the number of people who would pick up a product like this. Sure, your sales numbers probably won't be high – home goods stores, even small ones, will outsell you 10-1 – but it is a sales opportunity. Consider this: if you're using a linen (or terry or whatever) hand towel you are going to need a lot of them, so why not keep a handful back (30 or so towels wouldn't represent a large investment) as both backup towels to replace old ones and as stock for sale?

> **Fact**
>
> For many small items like towels, robes, moisturizer and lip balm, to name a few, you can have them branded with your logo, making them a product that promotes your brand and gives you some clout with your clients.

Moisturizer:

Like with soap, moisturizer offers an easy sales opportunity. Whether you get your moisturizer from local artisans and aromatherapy blenders, organic product distributors, importers, high-end domestic suppliers, or from somewhere else, if you put out a great product, your clients will want it, use it and want to take some home.

Makeup:

What woman hasn't gone to the powder room to freshen up? Take advantage of this habit and put out samples of makeup products from removers and cleansers to any of the makeup components you sell. If you give your clients the chance to use the products, it's more likely they'll want to buy. You probably already have samples available of many of your makeup products, so display them in the restroom and open up the opportunity for one more exposure to your clients.

Air Fresheners:

We all appreciate a fresh-smelling room (no matter what room it is), but candles or diffusers or other air fresheners would have too many smells to compete with on the salon floor. The best place for them is either the reception area (where you'll be displaying the product – of course – but may or may not be using them) or the restroom.

As with soap and moisturizers, you can find local artisans and aromatherapy blenders making essential oil blends, candles, tarts and more. Get some of their product, no matter what it is, and use it in your restroom. Face it, you need an air freshener in there anyway, you may as well be able to profit from its use. How do you display it? Easy: set up a shelf or counter area dedicated to your candle, diffuser, et cetera and the signage that goes with it, put it in a location that can't be missed and be sure to use scents that reflect the atmosphere of the salon (imagine trying to sell a hibiscus candle to a cutting-edge hipster salon customer).

Dressing Areas

If your salon offers spa treatments, you'll need a place for clients to change and store their personal items. In addition to providing adequate security for their personals and their modesty, you have a few selling opportunities in this area.

Think about what products your clients will use when getting ready for treatments.

- Robes or dressing gowns
- Slippers
- Air Fresheners

Air Fresheners:

As we mentioned just a couple of paragraphs ago, air fresheners can come from a variety of places, but in your dressing area they'll perform a different function from your restroom. In the dressing area, you want candles to relax and calm clients, setting them up for the treatment's they're about to receive or just received, in which case you'll be helping them enjoy their treatments for longer.

Robes:

Why not let your clients take home some of the luxury and relaxation they experienced at your salon? Robes and dressing gowns allow them to do just that. By having the clients change into robes before their treatment, you've added a step that helps put them in the mood for relaxation and you've wrapped them in something they can have at their home. Have a supply of robes for sale on hand in addition to those you're using in the spa. Be sure to have your logo and name embroidered on the robe.

Slippers:

Don't make your clients walk from the dressing area to the treatment room barefoot, give them the chance to slip into something soft, relaxing and easy on the feet. As with robes, you should have two sets of slippers – working slippers and a stock of sale slippers. Offer them in a relaxation package with a robe and a treatment as well as selling them by themselves. Not only are slippers a nice touch, they're also a nice small item to sell – they're perfect for hostess, mothers' day, birthday and holiday gifts (more on that strategy later).

THE PROS KNOW

"We place products on shelves at each station, but only products being used for specific services. We do this by knowing what the clients used for their last service. It makes for a very easy sale."

Chris Doanson
Mistic Hair, Tampa, FL

"The moment you walk in the salon, you are greeted by a receptionist who hands you a cover up branded with the Nordic Spa logo. I had a beautiful rug made for the entrance with the Nordic Spa logo also. When you leave my spa, you know exactly where you've been. Branding is everything."

Liz Vlvestad
Nordic Salons and Spas, Alexandria, VA

CHAPTER 14

A Bright Idea:
The Importance of Retailing Lighting

"A rooster crows only when it sees the light. Put him in the dark and he'll never crow. Show as many people the light and they will all crow."

—Muhammad Ali

Growing your retail business takes so many different steps to become successful. The location you choose to open your salon. The display cases you purchase to show of your products, trained and confident sales people that you and your customers can trust, and yes of course, the products you choose to sell.

So much can happen to drive or lose business, and that plays a huge impact on your business daily. The weather, a broken water main in the street that diverts traffic from your store or an unhappy employee that is turning off your customers from buying your products and the biggest thing in today world is the economy. These are things that sometimes are impossible to control and may be an act of God but there is certainly one thing we can do to make sure that our customers see the very best aspects of the products you sell by the lighting you use in your store.

Maintaining and growing a retail business means always showing off the best aspects of your products. Whether you sell shampoo, diamonds or doughnuts, you want your customers to look at the very best aspects of your products. The way you display them and the lighting you choose will set your store apart from the competitor down the street.

Most small retail stores forget the significance that lighting plays when attracting customers and stimulating them to buy. Have you thought about the importance of lighting when building your store? Most business owners get wrapped up in the fixtures that hold the product but not the lighting that actually lets your customers see what you are selling. The lighting fixtures you choose can have a big impact on customer impressions of your products. If you have the best retail products to sell in your store and people can't see them, you will not be successful at retailing.

Why Lighting is so Important

The first question that comes to mind is do you need light to run your business? Most store owners will agree without light it would be nearly impossible to run any type of business but how much and why is it so important? Common sense tells us that light is an integral part or a retail environment. The problem is most of us think that if we can flick a switch and the lights turn on we are open for business. That isn't necessarily the case; most of us take lighting for granted.

As, retailers, we have a business to run. Were consumed with the everyday duties of managing the store, employees, marketing, ordering inventory and dealing with customers. The thought of becoming a lighting specialist had never crossed your mind when you had the thought of opening your retail store.

Tips

If the customer can't see it, they can't buy it!

The key with lighting is you do not have to have a PhD in lighting just a little knowledge will go a long way. Non-technical people make lighting decisions every day. The trick is to know enough to make the right decisions. These decisions will improve employee productivity, retail sales, safety and security, identification and yes, your bottom line.

Key facts about inadequate lighting

- Consumers have a difficult time with colors they will pass up a purchase if they cannot decide if the color at your store is the one they will get at home.
- Customers need to be able to read the fine print.
- Customers need to see the price of an item.
- Employees may mismark an item or sku number.
- Employees may not realize stock is out and order new product or misplace and put in the wrong spot.
- Employees will take longer finding items that may be in a stock room without adequate light, leaving customers at the register.
- Employees may undercharge or overcharge your customers due to inadequate lighting at the point of checkout.
- Safety is always a a concern, so inside and outside your store, you must have adequate lighting.

Setting up your store lighting

When setting up your retail store, everything matters, from your choice of flooring to your display stands. One issue that you must prioritize when first designing your location is setting up your store for lighting. The lighting you use in your store can have a major effect on how the retail products or other items for sale look to customers. The best lighting for a retail store is and set of lights that make your products look attractive to shoppers. We recommend hiring a lighting professional if your electrician or architect cannot assist you with the lighting design for your retail store. Most electric supply stores will be able to assist you or recommend someone to help with your project.

Spotlights

If you plan to feature certain items or have a display case that you want to use in a specific area of the salon for hot new items or sale items spot light s can be very effective. A spotlight is an ideal way to draw attention to these specific items or area. The spotlight shines from the ceiling or wall toward its target. You can also install task or accent lighting, which puts a smaller spotlight on certain items on your selling floor, like items on a shelf or inside a cabinet.

LED Lighting

LED lighting fixtures offer a much more natural looking light, which can bring out the best in virtually any retail products. LEDs have been praised by many interior designers for providing the most authentic looking light, and you will find that neutral white LED's can provide the closest mirror to what an item would look like under bright, natural sunlight. When you want your customers to see you most intricate details of your retail items the best light to use to show of these products is the LED lights. LED simply cannot be beaten. Impressions matter greatly, and choosing the right fixtures can make all the difference.

Energy Efficient Recessed Lights

No matter what size your store is you must always consider your electric bill. If your retail store or salon is located in a mall you may be required to be open the same hours as the mall which is seven days a week and as much a 14 hour days. Your electric bill could be outlandish if you don't choose the right lighting. Since you often have to install a large number of lights at a retail location, look into energy efficient fixtures, recessed are the most popular.

Recessed fixtures sit within the ceilings of the store while standard fixtures hang and are sometimes adjustable. Energy efficient light fixtures contain lamps that use less energy compared to standard lighting options.

Natural Light

A retail store designer or a lighting expert will always suggest using natural light as a means to showing off your retail products' but in most cases there are to many obstacles to achieve that goal. If you are an interior store or inside a mall this will be difficult to accomplish. Natural lighting is the light that shines through the windows of your store from the sun or other lighting sources outside. This usually doesn't require anything you must simply make it a point to open all of your windows of the store each day to take advantage of the natural outside lights. The natural light is a great supplement to your artificial lighting.

The bottom line is that lighting makes a big difference in any retail outlet. Whether you are looking to move products or services or budget goods, the right lighting makes all the difference in the world. Investing in the correct lighting while designing your retail store is the most cost effective way to approach successful retailing.

Basic maintenance goes a long way

Improving your lighting system can be as easy as replacing the lamp or bulb. Many lamp types you may have inherited when you took over your retail space. Unfortunately, you may be stuck with because they are attached to the ceiling or walls and the cost would be too great to replace. The good news is the lighting industry has come a long way in the past few years. The lamp efficiency and brightness has increased dramatically. By replacing one lamp type with a more efficient version will enhance the light and also reduce your overall energy costs.

Lamps and luminaries, like any other surface, collect dust and dirt over time. When these lamp surfaces become dirty, they lose the luster and intensity of the light that they give off. They are working harder to give off the light they would normally give when clean. They become overheated and draw more energy, despite the poor quality of light they are giving off.

Bulbs lose their lumens with age and stop working as efficiently during the latter stages of their lives. We recommend group replacement. This involves replacing all the lamps in a retail store at the same time. This will guaranty the light levels in your retail store are above par at all times.

The lighting in your retail will slowly get worse overtime. It may not be noticeable but once you clean and or replace your bulbs, you will immediately notice a big difference.

Keeping a scheduled maintenance of cleaning or replacing the lights will keep your lighting at peak performance.

Cleaning your lighting fixtures and bulbs

1) Make sure your lights are off.
2) If using a ladder set to the side of the fixtures (do not set directly underneath a florescent bulb or light fixture). Fluorescents can easily come crashing down when slightly loosened. If you are standing to the side you will be out of danger.

Fact

While an abundance of natural light is desirable, a huge bank of windows can allow in a lot of heat and even create an unpleasant greenhouse effect inside. Consider UV blocking tinting or UV blocking, light diffusing shades to protect from the heat and damage long-term sun exposure brings.

3) Use a dusting cloth or large dust feather, if bulbs cannot be cleaned by dusting then replace them. We do not recommend using water on any bulbs or fluorescents. Electric and water to don't mix well. You may cause the bulb to blow up or even worse get electrocuted.

There are many lighting resources available to retail store owners. Most people get the bulk of the information from local lighting stores. These stores have sales people that are well versed in setting up stores or at least guiding you to make the right decisions when choosing your stores retail lighting.

Did You Know How Lighting Affects Your Clients?
- Lighting enhances the beauty of a product
- Lighting will change the feel and mood of a room – with harsh overhead lights, the room becomes intimidating, but with soft, diffused light from around the room, it becomes welcoming
- In your lighting makes your customers uncomfortable – either too bright and harsh or too dark – they will not stick around and spend money
- Accent lighting can put your customer in a buying mood by showing off new retail items
- Good lighting will aid your sales almost effortlessly by presenting products in an inviting way and putting your customers at ease

THE PROS KNOW

"The worst thing in your retail store are 'dark spots.' As a retailer, I know that if the customer can see it, they will pick it up, then it's up to my team to sell it. If clients can't see it, they keep walking and you have no chance at the sale."

Harrison Sasser
Gentlemen's Corner, Wilmington, NC

"I have almost 16' of retail. I use LED lighting that is the most brilliant white light on the market. And I have an expression in my salon: If a client is walking and talking through the retail area, they're not buyers, but the minute they stop, you've got them. Give them good lighting, let them see your products and they'll stop, buy and come back for more."

Juliann Gahr
Juliann's Styling Salon, Point Pleasant, NJ

"The most important lighting is over the guest. It makes them the star of the show. But your retail lighting needs to be bright and effective. We change bulbs regularly to maximize product visibility. Lighting can be the Achilles heel of your retail environment."

Chris Planson
Mistic Hair, Tampa, FL

"Lighting is the key to salon success. The better the lighting, the happier your clients. They'll see the correct color of their hair and get a real view of how great they look The correct lighting dynamics will change your hair color business and take your retail out of the shadows."

David Osgood
R.G. Skakoun Salons, Nashua, NH

Retail Tips Quick Reference Guide

Doorway to Wealth

- Keep your front entrance clean, neat and inviting.

- Give clients and passers by an idea of what to expect inside by what you show outside. This can be done with window treatments, signage and logo design, furnishings and fixtures.

- Create a funnel into your store. Wide, bare entryways are intimidating.

- Make your windows tell your story. They should sell beauty, hair, the services your clients want and the lifestyles they want to lead.

- Your windows should sell the products your clients want and the lifestyles they desire.

- Windows are a perfect display for featured, new or specialty products.

- All signage should be tasteful, with clear, legible lettering.

- Avoid script fonts at all costs, they're too hard to read.

- Avoid all caps, they're also too hard to read.

- Contrasting colors and textures create interest.

- Make sure your name is front and center. Clients should be able to easily see your name and identify what you do.

- Less is more when it comes to decorating your windows and entrance. Be tasteful, but not cluttered. Try following the old fashion rule: once you've accessorized, remove one item, then you're ready.

- Use a welcome mat of some sort in front of your front door.

---

10 Salon Design Considerations

A successful retail salon's layout communicates with the clients. The flow of traffic makes sense, the arrangement of retail items encourages interactions and sales, and the aesthetic and atmosphere communicates your brand message – affordable luxury, edgy, posh.

Along with the retail salon design considerations below, ask yourself the following: Does my layout encourage browsing and conversation with salon professionals about products? Does my layout draw customers deeper into the retail area? Does the arrangement of the store make it seem bigger than it is? Is my layout intuitive, and easy to understand and to navigate?

If you've answered "No" to any of these questions, reevaluate your retail salon's design and layout and find ways to improve the layout to encourage sales.

1. **Maximize the appearance of your retail salon.** Customers perceive a larger floor area with more stock, which they then associate with success and desirability. If you're in a small salon, there are ways to make it look bigger. Try to rearrange your aisles, putting more space between them. Adjust the shelves to be one or two stops higher. Flood the area with natural light.

2. **We read, and move, from left to right.** If you can, encourage your retail clients to flow through the retail area (and maybe the whole salon) from left to right. You can do this with the placement of your reception/check out desk in relation to your waiting area and retail zone.

3. **Design your layout with a grocery store in mind.** Grocery stores encourage you to visit every area of the store. How? Simple, by spreading out essentials – vegetables, deli, bread, eggs, butter and milk – across the floor, leading you from one to the other, showing you other items for sale along the way. Design your retail area in a similar way. Space out top-selling products to give your customers the chance to see other products for sale.

4. **Always display your retail products in a logical, orderly way.** In other words, be neat. You want customers to flow naturally through your retail area, not zigzag back on themselves to find complimentary items. Make it easy on them by grouping like items together. Think about a clothing store – active wear, underwear, formalwear and casual clothing are all grouped with similar items.

5. **Don't forget your checkout area.** Keep this area neat; allow for enough space to store the necessary equipment and items behind the counter and out of sight. Keep clutter to a minimum.

6. **Move your front desk deeper into the store.** It's called the front desk, but it doesn't have to be in the front. If you put it deeper into the store, you encourage clients to explore the salon's retail zone.

7. **Inspect.** Before you have a contractor come in to build out or install your retail zone, inspect the area and make sure you have adequate ventilation, lighting and electrical outlets. Communicate your needs clearly and in writing to the contractor and allow for any modifications you and your contractor deem necessary. After installation and build out, inspect again to ensure everything is in its place.

8. **Let your windows talk.** By hanging beauty images and displaying beautiful products in your windows, you communicate the idea that you're a salon, a place for beauty. An attractive window display is both inviting and enticing. You want your clients to see what's new, but you also want new clients to walk in the door.

9. **Don't allow your retail selection to look like a yard sale.** Table-height displays look like a yard sale, but bar-height tables and pedestals (generally 40" and above) make products look more attractive.

10. **Keep it neat.** Don't clutter your tables, pedestals, shelves and racks with unnecessary décor items. If you keep it neat, clean and simple, your product display will have a modern feel, which encourages buyers to buy.

THE PROS KNOW

"I have a small salon. The space is 1,000 square feet with six stylists. You enter the front of the salon under a trellis that places you right in the retail area. This puts the guest in the mood to understand they are in a professional coiffure. They don't go to the market to buy their hair products because they understand that we sell and are educated in retail. We have retail displayed everywhere in the salon."

Annamarie Lignori
Bellas Coiffures, Milan, Italy

Location Consideration

- Does the location have ample parking?
- Is it easy to pull in and out of the parking lot?
- Is there a traffic light or stop sign that may make it easier for clients to get in and out during high-traffic days?
- How much traffic drives by the location? (The Department of Transportation or city traffic department can often provide this information.)
- How much traffic walks by the location? (Though you want a loyal, returning client base, don't underestimate the buying power of walk-in clients, especially for your retail sales.)
- What are the shopping center's regulations on signage and exterior lighting?
- Does the city have ordinances over signage?
- What other businesses are nearby? (If you are looking for an upscale client, you should surround yourself with upscale stores. If you are looking for a family client base, you should find a location near other family-friendly dining and shopping destinations.)
- Is the area you're considering under good repair? Are sidewalks clean and unbroken, streetlights maintained, street and parking lot surface maintained and pothole free?
- How visible would your salon be from the street? From the parking lot?
- Is your location easy to find?
- Is the area safe at night?
- Do the price points, product lines and services of neighboring stories fall in line with what you offer?
- Do any of them compete directly with your retail or service offerings?
- Are the owners and employees friendly?

- What do they have to say about their location?
- How long will it take you to get to and from work? Are you comfortable with that commute?
- How close is your bank?
- Is there a place for you and employees to eat lunch affordably?
- If you need to take your kids to school, where are their school and afterschool programs located in relation to your salon?
- Have you identified the products you want to carry?
- Have you used the products and know their benefits and advantages?
- What products are available in your territory?
- Have you made contact with the sales representatives in your area?
- Are you aware of any product order minimums or restrictions associated with the products you want to carry?
- Have you decided on your salon's services, beauty treatments and spa treatments?
- Does your ideal location have enough space for the services, treatments, storage, retail and reception areas you desire?
- Can it be expanded (into the next storefront or by building onto the existing building) to fit your dream salon?
- Is there enough room for an effective retail area?
- Do you have enough storage space for stock and supplies?
- Is there room for a break room/employee lounge?

New Salon Checklist
For New Salon Owners

○ Define your business plan (goal setting, clientele, demographics, etc.).

○ Meet with your realtor.

○ Site location with good visibility and easy access.

○ Review preliminary lease. Is potential site zoned for a salon?

○ Prepare estimated annual income projection.

○ Preliminary budget plan.

○ Preliminary design and floor plan with supplier of furnishings, architect, or designer.

○ Inquire about and apply for the appropriate permits so your construction or remodeling can get underway without delay.

○ Design logo for salon (designer or graphic artist).

○ Write salon policies, employee and front desk manual.

○ Meet with your attorney to discuss setting up corporation and lease as well as items.

○ Meet with your banker to discuss items.

○ Meet with your accountant. Discuss purchase vs. leasing, bookkeeping vs. computer software, etc.

○ Select furnishings and color scheme for your salon.

○ Cash register, computer system or bookkeeping system.

○ Salon intercom and/or music system.

○ Finalize salon design and floor plan.

○ Pick out flooring, wall coverings, lighting, accent pieces, etc.

○ Meet with architect for complete set of plans. Salon meets all city and state codes.

○ Obtain bids for construction, usually with general contractor(s).

○ Sign lease, order salon furnishings and hire contractor(s).

○ Arrange for electric, gas, water, phone service and trash removal.

○ Plan opening date (make allowances for any delays).

○ Order dispensary and retail supplies and products.

○ Plan opening advertising (yellow pages, newspaper, direct mail, etc.).

○ Order magazines for customers.

○ Design and order outside sign in compliance with lease.

○ Order towels for shampoo area (special colors).

○ Salon price list on "Menu" of services.

○ Design customer sales tickets and service record files.

○ Order appointment cards, business cards, stamps and pads, stationary and envelopes.

○ Interview potential employees.

○ Order plants or plant service and outside doormats if applicable.

○ Order washer and dryer and laundry supplies or arrange for towel service.

○ Arrange for credit card charge plate machine or Merchant Processing with your bank.

○ Arrange for vending machines if applicable.

○ Purchase bookkeeping record books, appointment book, pencils, pens and stapler.

○ Purchase first aid kit, fire extinguisher, toilet paper and paper towel dispenser for restroom.

○ Purchase file cabinet, file folders, vacuum cleaner, broom and dust pan.

○ Purchase coffee bar supplies or arrange for coffee service.

○ Purchase ashtrays, waste baskets, cleaning supplies or arrange for cleaning service.

○ Plan Grand Opening – usually 30 days after opening.

○ Ongoing advertising, promotions and employee training.

PART IV

FURNITURE AND FIXTURES

CHAPTER 15

Retail at Every Turn: The Right Units for the Right Zones

"A person is born with a liking for profit."

—Xun Zi

In order to maximize your salon's profit potential retail is a must. It allows you to sell not only products, but also additional services. It allows you to position your salon (and you and your employees) as the authority on beauty. It allows for additional income, a boost to your salon's reputation and even happier, more loyal clients.

Retail is the perfect compliment to your salon treatments, but only if it's done right. To do it right, you need to display your products in the right way. In this chapter, we'll look at retail display units by area and go into more depth on what types of display units you can get.

Zone By Zone

Reception

The reception counter is more than just the place to schedule appointments, check in and pay; it's a command center and a selling opportunity. As we stated in previous chapters, reception and retail zones should be close in proximity; after all, if clients have to wait, make them wait in front of products they'll want to purchase and use.

In the reception area – your checkout counter, desk or table – you'll have space to display a few small items. In grocery stores, these are called impulse items. They're high profit margin, relatively low priced items, and it's a trend that's carried over into standard retail shops. Think about Victoria's Secret and Bath & Body Works. These stores funnel customers through towers, racks and rows of small, easy to buy, relatively cheap items. How many times have you seen someone in line (or maybe you were that someone) pick up a lipstick, perfume sampler or lotion from the rack and add another $3-5 to their purchase? Now think of how many clients walk out your door without paying for more than a salon treatment and tip.

The area immediately around the counter is the perfect place for a small table or tower display. Freestanding towers are often more expensive than pedestals (on the lower end, think of $200-$500 for a tower and $100-$300 for a pedestal) but tables are more expensive than towers (think of a price and you can find a table or set of nesting tables for that much and more).

Don't forget the counter top. This is a perfect place for a final retail push. Counter space is at a premium – you'll want to be able to have at least two people at the counter (one coming, one going) at the same time, so space is tight – which means you'll have to be selective with what type of unit you use there. Reasonably priced display units, like spinning countertop units perfect for holding travel-sized hair products, makeup and other similar small items can cost as little as $50 new, but more ornate or complex countertop displays (whether they're a spinning rack, riser or something else) can be very expensive – think well over $200.

Square footage is valuable and you don't want to crowd the customer with retail, you want them to have room to breathe and have a pleasant experience in your salon after all, so selecting the right units is crucial when it comes to traffic flow. There's a balance to strike between smooth movement of people within the space and an aggressive (but not overtly aggressive) retail offering. We recommend a tower (spinning or fixed shelves), a pedestal and a countertop display That combination works in most salons and provides you with enough space to effectively put some of those impulse purchases into the hands of your clients.

Retail – The Shopping Zone

Your retail zone will feature the biggest cluster of display units and products. The style of the retail units should fit the style of the salon, and there are a lot of options available for purchasing display pieces, putting chic retail units within any budget's reach.

Bookcases

Bookcases come in many widths and tend to be both durable and attractive. Many are 7' tall and 3'-4' wide, although other sizes are available depending on where you source your bookcases. Size isn't the only option; you'll need to look at color, finish, lighting, storage options (you can put doors on the bottom of many bookcases to create storage), assembly and installation.

At IKEA, the Swedish home goods store, they sell a wide array of bookcases for the home, many of which would be suitable for use in a salon, as well as providing design consultation services and special product lines for business customers. Their Billy bookcases offer traditional shelving options, but are easy to put together and durable enough for two to three year's heavy use. Billy bookcases come in four colors and start at $79 for a 6'5" unit that is 31.5" wide.

IKEA also carries more contemporary and even modern solutions. Their Lack wall shelf ($49) is ultra-modern and comes in crisp red, black and white colors and are sure to become a focal point of your salon's retail area. The Vittsjö shelving units ($40 for single towers, $70 for doubles) have glass shelves and a metal body for a sleek, contemporary look that's at home in any salon. The Vittsjö shelves are also open all the way around, making them ideal for display from any angle or for display against a mural or wall hanging.

If a modern, edgy look is your thing, check out IKEA's Expedit system (starting a $149 for a 5' x 5' unit). Expedit comes in high gloss red, white and gray, as well as several non-gloss colors, and is a grid rather than a traditional shelving system. Four vertical and horizontal dividers make 16 cubes perfect for retail display in an interesting, inviting and chic space.

Styling Floor and Salon Services

On the styling floor, you'll want to keep your retail displays simple. Pedestals, which we mentioned earlier, work well to display small groups of products. The IKEA Expedit system could work as a retail display and station divider, though they may take up more floor space than you'd like. Another solution is shelves. A variety of glass shelves (which are stylish and go with almost any salon décor) are available from a variety of retailers. Here are a few popular options.

IKEA

IKEA has several glass shelf options with prices ranging from $12.99-$24.99.

- The Framstå ($20) and Linjal ($24.99) mount to the wall via an aluminum track and appear to float.

- Grundtal ($14.99) has a more industrial look with two metal brackets supporting the shelf.

- Baren ($12.99) features tempered glass and is ideal for heavier loads (when properly installed).

- Lillholmen ($19.99) has a more traditional look.

Home Depot

Aside from a couple of the IKEA options, Home Depot has our favorite shelves. Prices at Home Depot vary wildly, from $16.99-$258.

- The Wallscapes Allure ($68.96) is one of our favorite products. A bent shelf, it gives you two levels (so you can feature products differently), appears to float, and is strong enough for retail display. It would add visual interest to a grouping of similar floating glass shelves.

  Selection and availability will vary by location, so check with someone in the bathroom or home décor departments for options and additional products that may require a special order. This just gives you a starting point for your budget.

Lowes

Options at Lowes are more limited than those from Home Depot, and the price point is very similar. Many of the brands are the same and the product lines are very close in style.

- The Kingston Milano Glass Shelf ($60.97) is one of our favorites here. The hardware comes in a variety of finishes (satin nickel, oil rubbed bronze) and the shelf has softly curved face, for visual interest.

You may also want to contact a local glass and mirror shop, they will have options for shelves and shelving systems that may appeal more to your style. As a local small business, many may be willing to work out pricing breaks or deals with another small business.

Spa

In your spa and treatment rooms (for manicures, facials, et cetera), you'll probably want something more casual and comfortable; something that looks like it came from a chic home. That's why we recommend looking at home furnishing stores, specifically stores like IKEA, Pier 1, Costplus World Market and local antique/resale shops. Since your spa treatment areas will only be home to a few pieces of furniture, it's important to get a lot of value out of each piece.

In your massage therapy rooms, you'll have a massage table and maybe a massage chair, a chair, a table for your client's belongings, and some sort of wardrobe/hutch to store sheets, towels and massage oils (gels or foams or whatever you use). What about hot or cold stone treatments? What about aromatherapy? What about music? It's easy to integrate the stone warmers/chillers and oil diffusers into a piece of furniture. The same with your sound system.

Picture this: a tall piece of furniture with doors on the bottom, a counter top and then shelves above. Below you have space for storing extra supplies. On the counter, you have room for a stone warmer (the chiller, it may have to go into the bottom, but installing it there is no problem for an experienced carpenter) and a small sound system (there are a lot of great MP3 player-compatible systems that will work very well in a spa setting). Plus, the shelves give you space for a small retail display (the aromatherapy oils and candles, massage oils, other small relaxation items) and a spot to keep a spare massage oil in easy reach.

In other areas within you spa, like a Vichy shower room or facial treatment area, you'll have different needs. Be aware of the different finished and products furniture is made of. You don't want something that can't get wet near the shower, and you have to be mindful of the wear and tear the furniture will receive during use.

Take a look at PureSpaDirect.com, they carry a lot of great options for your spa furniture, fixtures and equipment, as well as pieces for your restrooms and dressing areas.

Restrooms and Dressing Areas

Your restrooms and dressing areas are much like the spa rooms – you'll want to look at more home décor and home furnishing stores for pieces like vanities and chairs, but you'll need to look elsewhere for lockers. Yes, we said lockers. If your clients disrobe in a central area rather than in a room, you'll need to securely hold their belongings. Lockers can also be useful for storing cleaning supplies behind a locked door.

Take a look at what your local hardware store, like Lowes or Home Depot, has by way of bathroom vanities. Also find local kitchen and bath cabinet centers (like Marcraft) for more options.

For your dressing area, PureSpaDirect.com has a large assortment of lockers and furniture in a range of styles.

In these areas, your retail section will be small. For restrooms, space is a major consideration. If you have room, a small table (like a sofa table, tall, skinny and long) or set of glass shelves (like the ones between styling stations) will give you enough room to showcase an item or two. In your dressing areas, you may want to sell through experience – like letting clients know the plush robe they're wearing is available to take home – or directly – with a table display or shelves as in the restroom.

CHAPTER 16

Pricing Your Custom Retail Furniture

In the previous chapter, we mentioned several commercial companies that carry different types of generic shelving units for retail or storage. What if you feel that these units don't fit your décor and you want something different? What do you do? Where do you go? You can begin by looking at the Internet, where you can find everything, but it can be quite overwhelming. This chapter will help narrow your search, give you pointers to look for and an approximate price of what you should be paying.

Any cabinet manufacturer can make units to order. The units can be any size, shape, depth, height and style you desire. Of course, with that in mind, this made to order unit can get quite expensive. If you are using any manufacturer that does not have much retail experience, we recommend that you sit with their designer so you have input and can let them know what product is going on the shelves and how you want to present it.

We have mentioned in previous chapters of companies that specialize in beauty cabinets and have a better understanding of what you need. Here are a few companies that are direct manufacturers with a lot of retail experience

- Collins Mfg.
- Minerva Beauty
- Salon Interiors
- Salon Centric
- Takara Belmont
- Kaemark

You can give them a drawing for them to price out or you can have them design a unit to your liking.

When designing your unit, here are a few things to look for:

- **Shelving.** We recommend a glass shelf for all units, especially if lighting is coming from above. The glass shelf should be clear, tempered glass with a polished edge finish. If you are just using the sides of the unit with shelf clips to support the shelf, we suggest that it is no longer than 36", although 24" units are preferable due to the size, weight and expense of the glass. Also, the thickness of the glass shelf needs to be at least 3/8". Anything thinner than that has the potential to break because of the weight it handles.

There are two main ways to support the shelves: from the back with shelf brackets, or shelf clips from the side. Brackets on the back are unsightly, so we recommend that you use the adjustable shelf clips used on the sides. These clips are supported on the side by metal grommets that reinforce its stability.

- **Lighting.** Most retail units have a soffit that at the top part of the cabinet. The usual height of that part is 8 to 10 inches, which is plenty of room to install lighting (and even speakers) and wiring. Most cabinetmakers use a "recessed hi hat" light that is drilled through the bottom of the soffit for direct lighting.

  A few things to keep in mind. Lights need electricity, so there needs to be a junction box located at the top of the retail unit. A standard height of a retail unit is 7 feet. So, the electrical junction box needs to be at 88" off the floor. This will put the electric connection just above the unit. All depending on your cabinet person, the lights can just be a plug in or need to be "hard wired" (wired directly into the wall, like a standard light fixture); if you ever plan to rearrange and move your retail units, you'll need to consider this. Either way, the outlet needs to be connected to an on/off switch. That can be handled two ways: a switch can be installed and wired on the retail unit, or it can be installed on the wall somewhere near the cabinet.

  Lighting is very important for retail. Without it, you do not properly highlight the area and will lose sales. If you buy an existing salon, they may have a retail area without lighting. Our suggestion is to add directional spotlight to the unit for highlighting. This will increase sales and your bottom line.

- **Construction of your retail unit.** Building a retail unit is a specialized field and the company that provides your units must know their stuff about retail. The cabinetmaker that you choose may do excellent work and he could have built your kitchen cabinets, but does he know how to build a retail unit? Here are some pointers to keep in mind.

  Retail units can extend along a wall 6, 9 or even 12 feet. Cabinet manufacturers usually make it in sections at those lengths. We recommend that each section be no longer than 36". The reason for that is the shelving that the product sits on. Product can get very heavy, especially if you have 20 to 30 items sitting on the shelf. That means you can have 25 to 40 pounds resting on the glass shelf. You will see a bow in the shelf if it is longer than 36" and it will look unsightly and be at risk of breaking. Slimmer units, 24"-30", give you more stability and an attractive look and may be the best option, especially if you're displaying heavy items.

  Now that we are making this unit in sections, the construction of the unit is very important. Many cabinetmakers use 5/8" particleboard in building their product. This wood is the most cost effective approach and, believe it or not, it's one of the easiest to work with. As long as there is no water involved, particleboard is the cheapest building material to use. Many people want plywood, but unless you use a "top grade" plywood, it can be difficult to work with and much more expensive.

When you cabinet builder is assembling each section, most use only the 5/8" particleboard on the sides. Once they bring it to the location, they screw it together to create one unit. There are two reasons not to do that. One, with the floor not being level (99% of the time) it is almost impossible to line up each side together to create one clean joint. The finished product, when assembled, is unsightly and unprofessional. Second, with the uneven floor, the units don't line up on the top and bottom, so when you view the unit from afar, the shelves don't line up from one unit to another. We recommend designing the unit with an overlay cap, where one side fits over the other and there is no seam. This is a very simple way to give it a professional look.

Tips

> Doors on products, even glass doors, mean "Do Not Touch!" Never put retail items you intend to sell behind glass.

- **Glass doors.** Glass doors are only used for security and not an effective way to sell retail. A client must touch and feel the product when buying it. We do not recommend this for your salon. If you do decide to put them on your unit, the price for a pair of locking glass doors would be $200-300 dollars.

Here are some prices so you can budget for your next project. When figuring out a price, it is usually done by linear footage, so if a unit is 6 feet long, then it would be the price per foot times six.

Price per foot

Basic retail unit	$150 per foot
Mid Range unit	$300 per foot
High End unit	$600 per foot

Of course, you can spend a lot more per foot if you are using special material, stainless steel or some expensive material. This just gives you a starting point to go from.

When using standard materials, prices will reflect the quality of the materials and craftsmanship, and often be a clue to the durability and sturdiness of the furniture.

6 foot unit Basic	$900.00
6 foot Mid Range	$1,800.00
6 foot High End	$3,600.00

Furnishing your salon can be expensive. In the next chapter, we'll go over some estimated costs to help you get your budget lined out.

When ordering your salon furniture and equipment did you:

- Select a durable product for high-use areas like workstations?

- Select a styling chair that is practical (comfortable for customers, affordable for you, complimentary to the salon's style)?

- Select reception furnishings that fit the salon's style and provided adequate space for the job?

- Identify and install plenty of retail display cases that fit with your salon's style and budget?

- Remember the back rooms – break room furniture and storage, as well as overstock furniture and storage?

- Select durable, reliable equipment for your treatment and service areas (massage tables, pedicure stations, et cetera).

- Install an appropriate shampoo backwash unit?

- Allow for adequate ventilation in areas where hair coloring and other chemical treatment will take place?

- Line up the appropriate trades people (electrician, plumber, carpenter) to assist with installation?

THE PROS KNOW

"We have a lot of great advice to pass along: Having a central retail area on or near the counter is a must for merchandise impulse buys during checkout. Stylists must be using the 'product of the month' while cutting and styling hair. Removing old posters and promotional material and replacing them with new, fresh posters and pictures helps keeps the style of the salon current. Display product everywhere, which reminds the clients of the brands we carry and the products they can use to look and feel better. Use a mobile merchandising cart and move it every day."

Sharron Barajas
Woody's Marketing Manager, Los Angeles, CA

CHAPTER 17

Furniture and Equipment Pricing

Not all salons are created equal, but they do require the same basic equipment. These tables show you a budget for a four-, six- and eight-station salon at three different price levels. Your prices may vary based on finishes, colors, location and style, so let these serve as a guide when making your allowances for furnishing your salon.

Budget Style Salon–Furniture & Equipment Pricing Breakdown

	Per Unit	4-Station	6-Station	8-Station
Styling chair	$175.00	$700.00	$1,050.00	$1,400.00
Dryer chair	$350.00	$1,400.00	$1,400.00	$1,400.00
Sink	$175.00	$350.00	$525.00	$700.00
Shampoo chair	$125.00	$250.00	$375.00	$500.00
Reception desk	$400.00	$400.00	$400.00	$600.00
Retail unit	$250.00	$250.00	$250.00	$500.00
Reception chairs	$80.00	$320.00	$320.00	$480.00
Nail table	$140.00	$280.00	$280.00	$280.00
Styling Station	$150.00	$600.00	$900.00	$1,200.00
Mirror	$75.00	$300.00	$450.00	$600.00
Pedicure unit	$600.00	$600.00	$600.00	$1,200.00
Stool	$75.00	$225.00	$225.00	$300.00
Shampoo cabinet	$300.00	$600.00	$900.00	$1,200.00
Color trolley	$80.00	$320.00	$480.00	$640.00
Shipping		$1,500.00	$2,200.00	$3,000.00
	TOTALS	**$8,095.00**	**$10,355.00**	**$14,000.00**

NOTES:

DRYER: for a six- and eight-station salon, only four dryers are usually needed.

SINK: for a six-station salon, three sinks; for an eight-station salon, four sinks.

RECEPTION DESK: for the eight-station salon, a larger desk is needed.

RETAIL UNIT: for a six-station salon, at least one additional retail unit is recommended. Estimate also does not include retail display units (like wall shelves) between stations and any bins or baskets you may want.

RECEPTION CHAIR: for an eight-station salon, six chairs are recommended.

PEDICURE UNIT: a second unit is recommended for an eight-station setup.

STOOL: a fourth stool is recommended for the additional pedicure unit.

SPA: spa units (like massage tables and specialized treatments like hot or cold stones, Vichy showers, and the like were not included) but can be considerable investments.

Additional Service Furniture & Equipment (Optional)

Makeup station	$400.00
Makeup chair	$200.00
Facial table	$400.00
Multifunction facial unit	$700.00
TOTALS	**$1,700.00**

Mid-Range Style Salon–Furniture & Equipment Pricing Breakdown

	Per Unit	4-Station	6-Station	8-Station
Styling chair	$400.00	$1,600.00	$2,400.00	$3,200.00
Dryer chair	$600.00	$2,400.00	$2,400.00	$2,400.00
Sink and chair unit	$700.00	$1,400.00	$1,400.00	$2,100.00
Reception desk	$1,000.00	$1,000.00	$1,500.00	$2,000.00
Retail unit	$900.00	$900.00	$900.00	$1,800.00
Reception chair	$200.00	$800.00	$800.00	$1,20.00
Nail table	$400.00	$800.00	$800.00	$800.00
Styling Station	$500.00	$2,000.00	$3,000.00	$4,000.00
Mirror	$150.00	$600.00	$900.00	$1,200.00
Pedicure unit	$2,500.00	$2,500.00	$2,500.00	$5,000.00
Stool	$150.00	$300.00	$300.00	$450.00
Shampoo cabinet	$600.00	$1,200.00	$1,200.00	$1,800.00
Color trolley	$150.00	$600.00	$900.00	$1,200.00
Shipping		$2,000.00	$2,600.00	$3,500.00
	TOTALS	**$18,100.00**	**$21,600.00**	**$30,650.00**

NOTES:

DRYER: for a six- and eight-station salon, only four dryers are usually needed.

SINK: for a six-station salon, three sinks; for an eight-station salon, four sinks.

RECEPTION DESK: for the eight-station salon, a larger desk is needed.

RETAIL UNIT: for a six-station salon, at least one additional retail unit is recommended. Estimate also does not include retail display units (like wall shelves) between stations and any bins or baskets you may want.

RECEPTION CHAIR: for an eight-station salon, six chairs are recommended.

PEDICURE UNIT: a second unit is recommended for an eight-station setup.

STOOL: a fourth stool is recommended for the additional pedicure unit.

SPA: spa units (like massage tables and specialized treatments like hot or cold stones, Vichy showers, and the like were not included) but can be considerable investments.

Additional Service Furniture & Equipment (Optional)

Makeup station	$1,000.00
Makeup chair	$300.00
Facial table	$1,200.00
Multifunction facial unit	$1,500.00
TOTALS	**$4,000.00**

High-End Style Salon—Furniture & Equipment Pricing Breakdown

	Per Unit	4-Station	6-Station	8-Station
Styling chair	$1,200.00	$4,800.00	$7,200.00	$9,600.00
Dryer chair	$1,000.00	$4,000.00	$4,000.00	$4,000.00
Sink and chair unit	$2,500.00	$5,000.00	$7,500.00	$10,000.00
Reception desk	$3,000.00	$3,000.00	$3,500.00	$4,000.00
Retail unit	$2,000.00	$2,000.00	$2,000.00	$4,000.00
Reception chair	$400.00	$1,600.00	$1,600.00	$2,400.00
Nail table	$800.00	$800.00	$800.00	$800.00
Styling Station	$2,000.00	$8,000.00	$12,000.00	$16,000.00
Mirror	$300.00	$1,200.00	$1,800.00	$2,400.00
Pedicure unit	$5,000.00	$5,000.00	$2,500.00	$5,000.00
Stool	$300.00	$600.00	$600.00	$900.00
Shampoo cabinet	$1,200.00	$1,200.00	$1,200.00	$1,200.00
Color trolley	$400.00	$2,400.00	$900.00	$640.00
Color lab	$8,000.00	$8,000.00	$8,000.00	$8,000.00
Color chairs (2)	$800.00	$1,600.00	$1,600.00	$1,600.00
Color stations (2)	$1,500.00	$3,000.00	$3,000.00	$3,000.00
Dispensary	$2,500.00	$2,500.00	$2,500.00	$3,000.00
Makeup unit	$2,500.00	$2,500.00	$2,500.00	$2,500.00
Makeup chair	$500.00	$500.00	$500.00	$500.00
Facial table	$3,500.00	$3,500.00	$3,500.00	$3,500.00
Facial unit	$2,500.00	$2,500.00	$2,500.00	$2,500.00
Microdermabrasion	$3,000.00	$3,000.00	$3,000.00	$3,000.00
Vichy shower	$4,000.00	$4,000.00	$4,000.00	$4,000.00
Hydrotherapy tub	$3,500.00	$3,500.00	$3,500.00	$3,500.00
Color Processor	$2,200.00	$2,200.00	$2,200.00	$2,200.00
Shipping		$3,500.00	$4,000.00	$5,000.00
TOTALS		**$79,820.00**	**$93,980.00**	**$109,040.00**

NOTES:

DRYER: for a six- and eight-station salon, only four dryers are usually needed.

SINK: for a six-station salon, three sinks; for an eight-station salon, four sinks.

RECEPTION DESK: for the eight-station salon, a larger desk is needed.

RETAIL: for an eight-station salon, a second retail unit is recommended.

RECEPTION CHAIR: for an eight-station salon, six are recommended.

PEDICURE UNIT: a second one is recommended for a high-end salon.

STOOL: a fourth stool for the additional pedicure unit.

continued

Additional Service Furniture & Equipment (Optional)

Makeup station	$1,000.00
Makeup chair	$300.00
Facial table	$1,200.00
Multifunction facial unit	$1,500.00
TOTALS	**$4,000.00**

Don't forget to factor in installation, which can run from $300-$1,000 (or more!) per day, depending on the skills, tools and number of workers you need.

Pricing it Out

In previous chapters we mentioned several places to go for low-cost, but stylish, retail displays, reception furnishings and checkout counters/desks (like IKEA), but what about the salon- and spa-specific equipment? Our advice: take it to the Internet. Here are several sites we found that have used and new salon equipment.

- **Craigslist.org** – This online yard sale has everything from cars to condos and many businesses use their search feature to look for "salon chair" and other pieces of equipment in their "for sale" section.

- **MinervaBeauty.com** – New, sale and clearance salon furniture in a variety of price ranges and styles.

- **HairStylersFriend.com** – Used salon equipment at reasonable prices. Selections vary, so check in from time to time if you don't see what you need.

- **SalonInteriors.com** – An assortment of new and used salon and spa equipment and fixtures. Made on the premises using products from the United States.

- **CollinsMfgCo.com** – Quality at its best. Another fine U.S.-based manufacturer.

- **TakaraBelmont.com** – Manufacturing salon equipment for more than 85 years.

- **Ebay.com** - Sellers on this online auction giant carry a variety of new and used salon equipment.

Why do you want to look at craigslist and other online outlets? To save money. Take a look at this chart. The prices here are estimates based on what we found on the market when researching this book, so use this only as a rough guide for used salon and spa furniture.

Furniture Comparison

	Budget		Expensive	
	Used	New	Used	New
Styling chairs	$75.00	$175.00	$200.00	$1,200.00
Dryer chairs	$150.00	$350.00	$200.00	$1,000.00
Sink	$75.00	$175.00	$175.00	$400.00
Shampoo chair	$50.00	$125.00	$125.00	$350.00
Reception desk	$150.00	$400.00	$400.00	$2,000.00
Retail unit	$100.00	$250.00	$300.00	$900.00
Reception chairs	$25.00	$80.00	$100.00	$400.00
Nail table	$50.00	$140.00	$125.00	$800.00
Styling stations	$50.00	$150.00	$200.00	$2,00.00
Clothes washer	$100.00	$400.00	NA	NA
Clothes dryer	$100.00	$400.00	NA	NA
Pedicure unit	$200.00	$600.00	$500.00	$5,000.00
Stools	$25.00	$75.00	$50.00	$200.00
Facial steamer	$75.00	$180.00	$150.00	$450.00
Magnifying lamp	$50.00	$200.00	$150.00	$500.00
Facial table	$75.00	$200.00	$300.00	$3,500.00
Multi-function unit	$200.00	$600.00	$300.00	$2,000.00
Sink vanity	$50.00	$200.00	$150.00	$500.00
Shampoo cabinet	$100.00	$300.00	$200.00	$1,200.00
Shampoo unit	$150.00	$500.00	$400.00	$2,000.00
Make up unit	$50.00	$200.00	$250.00	$2,500.00
Color trolley	$25.00	$80.00	$75.00	$400.00
TOTALS	**$1,925.00**	**$5,730.00**	**$4,300.00**	**$27,300.00**

Tips for Buying Salon Equipment:

1. When shopping online, make sure you buy from a reputable company. Read customer reviews and comments, they'll reveal a lot about the quality of the product and customer service.

2. Check the dimensions of what you're buying and make sure units and components will fit through a standard 36" door opening.

3. Salon equipment is very heavy, you'll need help opening boxes and putting pieces in place.

4. When ordering shelving, anything more than 48" will require a support in the middle, otherwise you'll have sagging shelves. Stick with cabinets that are less than 36".

5. When buying online, remember that what you see is not always what you get. Check the return policies before you buy and ship anything to your salon. You may have to pay to return items (and that's not cheap).

THE PROS KNOW

"The designer I used through the whole process of building my salon reminded me daily of the importance of building a beautiful reception and retail area. I am in a very busy strip mall and people stop and look into my windows often. Many times, they'll come in just to tell me how beautiful the salon is; we send most of them on their way with a thank you, some product they've purchased and an appointment to come back for a service."

Stephen Sanders
Epic Salons, Las Vegas, NV

PART V

SALES AND MARKETING

CHAPTER 18

Why Buy?

Awell-designed retail area is only a small part of the retail sales process. Sure, if you have your products displayed neatly you'll sell a few, but how do you sell a lot? By understanding consumer behavior and knowing how to turn browsers into buyers, that's how.

Why Do Your Clients Buy?

Before you look at your clients, look at yourself. Why do you buy? You buy for a lot of reasons. Take a look at this list and mark all the reasons you've ever bought anything.

○ Because owning or using a product makes you feel good.

○ Because you've had good experience with the product (or something similar) in the past.

○ Because of the brand's reputation.

○ Because of the prestige of owning or using a product.

○ Because you liked the way it looked/felt/smelled/tasted/sounded.

○ Because your friend owned one.

○ Because it supported the lifestyle you have or want to have.

○ Because it helps you express your identity.

○ Because owning or using a product helps make you look better.

○ All of the above.

How many of you said "All of the above?" We know we did. Why? Because there are different needs, wants and motivations to buy at different times. Sometimes you impulse buy because you want a product in the moment. Sometimes you research and make the decision-making process very long. Sometimes a salesperson shows you the benefits of a product and you see how it fits.

There are a number of reasons your clients will buy services and products from your salon.

- Clients buy to reinforce self-concepts and self-image (it makes them look and feel good)
- Clients buy to maintain their lifestyle or the appearance of their lifestyle (it puts them on par with or above their peers)
- Clients buy to impress their peer groups
- Clients buy to express their individuality and identity

And a number of internal and external factors influence their purchases.

- Client's mood
- Experience with product in the past
- Trust (in the product and in your salon)
- Convenience
- Emotions
- Personality
- How they view themselves
- Household structure
- Cultural beliefs

That's an overview of why clients buy but why do they buy from you, when do they buy and what's the purchase process like?

Clients buy from businesses that make them feel at home. They're happy to be in the business and happy to give them money. **Solution:** Always be welcoming, friendly, warm and take the extra step to ensure a client's happiness.

Clients buy from sales people who know their product. **Solution:** Be sure your staff knows and uses the products they're selling and that they know how to talk about them.

Finances, household structures and pay cycles determine clients' consumption patterns. **Solution:** Offer a variety of products across the price spectrum (within reason), package products for discounts and offer loyalty programs on products and services.

Clients go through a complicated decision-making process before they purchase. They weigh internal and external factors before finalizing that sale. **Solution:** Know the basics of consumer buying habits and sell using that knowledge. By knowing your customer, you'll be able to really home in on what they want and need and be able to sell to them more effectively.

How We Decide

The decision-making process is made up of five steps. That's all that lays between your customer and a sale.

The Decision-Making Process

1. A *need* is triggered in the consumer by internal or external factors.
2. A *search* for a solution to the need takes place.
3. The options undergo *evaluation* and are narrowed down.
4. A *purchase* is made based on the need, search and evaluation.
5. An *assessment* of the product and process is made after the purchase. This helps determine future purchases of the same product or from the same place.

Need

In the first step, the client recognizes they have a need. Internal or external forces can trigger this need. Internal needs are easier to think of as wants or desires – "I am unhappy with they way my hair looks and need a new style and products;" where external needs are easier to think of as physical issues with a solution (though external needs aren't just physical) – "My makeup dries out my skin and I need something better" or "I want to fit in with my peers/the current hair trend, so I need to get this trendy hair style."

- Internal forces are those things within your client that leads them to take an action – they're hungry, so they eat; they're tired, so they sleep. In your salon these internal needs will be tied to vanity, beauty and self-image.
- External forces are those outside influences that get you to take an action. Dry skin; a brush, dryer or beauty tool they're unhappy with; the need to keep up with their peers.

Your clients will identify their needs in several ways.
- Through a conversation with a friend or by seeing an ad or display that causes them to recognize their need.
- Through self-discovery and self-awareness.
- With the help of an educated sales person.

As a retail salon, your job is to capitalize on needs in all three phases.

- **Show** clients the products and how they provide solutions. Displays, ads and signage works well here.

- **Demonstrate** how a product provides a solution and go for a softer sales approach. An example of this would be styling someone's hair while talking to them casually and naturally about how easy this is to do at home if you have the right tools and product.

- **Listen** to what they're saying and they'll tell you what they need, whether they know it or not, then provide a solution with the proper product or service.

Search and Research

The second step involves doing research to find a solution that fits their need, budget, lifestyle and desires. With major purchases – think cars, homes, expensive electronics – this phase can take quite a long time, but with minor purchases – groceries, clothes, beauty products – the time is much shorter, though it varies by product and personality.

This phase has two steps: heightened awareness and a search for information. Think of them as passive and active searching.

- During *passive searching*, your client has recognized a need and is keeping their eyes and ears open for solutions. They pay more attention to ads, product mentions, displays, demonstrations and may conduct some very light research (internet search or asking her friends).

- During *active searching*, your client invests time and energy into learning more about solutions to their needs. Asking experts (like your salon employees) for advice and recommendations, polling friends in a more thorough manner and doing some in-depth Internet research are examples of active searching.

Keep in mind where your clients will turn for information and where you want them to turn for information. They'll go to:

- Family, friends, neighbors and acquaintances
- Groups they belong to where there may be a mix of friends and acquaintances – mommy groups, church groups, gym classes, coffee shops
- Ads, salespeople, product literature (print and online)
- Product experts and daily users
- Consumer guides and other stories, positive and negative
- Online sources like Web forums, blogs and product websites
- A place they can try the product themselves – dressing rooms, sample stations, shows, classes, demonstrations, a friend's house

Where do you want them to turn? You.

Become the expert they turn to first. Your salon, your stylists, your retail section, your website and everything about your salon should be a resource for them. They should be able to find their information in nearly every phase of the gathering process from you.

Evaluation

After searching and researching their needs and possible solutions, the next step is the evaluation of their options. In this stage, all the benefits and features of the product are weighed against the identified need. In plain English – the consumer looks at what the product delivers as compared to what they want it to do. When they find a match, they move on to assessing the value and purchasing.

Clients will approach evaluation differently. Some will use logic, almost like they have a checklist or set of rules; others will use emotions and see how a thing "feels;" and still others will buy based strictly on the performance of the product.

To capitalize on selling opportunities, your employees need to know the features and benefits of your product line and be able to help clients through the evaluation process. By answering questions, giving opinions and providing factual product information, your employees can make this process shorter, easier and lead into the purchase of the product.

Part of helping this process along is to provide alternatives to combat objections. If they don't like this product because it's too expensive, offer a lower-cost alternative or demonstrate the benefits in a different way to illustrate the value of the product ("I know this dye is more expensive, but if we use it, you'll only need five treatments a year, not six, which is better for your hair and it comes out to save you money at the end of the year.").

When your clients are evaluating the product, the value is a key area they'll look. Too many clients value = price, but really value = price x performance. You have to ensure that you and your employees provide real value, not just in the product but in support as well. If you sell them on a beauty tool they don't know how to use, they'll never use it and speak poorly about it and you.

There are two major factors at play during the last part of the evaluation phase: when will they buy and where will they buy? As for when, you want that answer to be now; as for where, you want that answer to be here. What impacts these decisions and drives a customer to buy from you rather than Amazon (where, no doubt) they can find the product cheaper and now rather than later?

Several things influence the decision to buy, from the store atmosphere to the pressure they get from sales staff. Push too hard and they'll shy away. Don't press hard enough and they'll walk out. One way to increase the pressure to buy is with incentives. Sales, packages, bundles and loyalty programs all help you apply gentle pressure to buy because they all offer added value to the purchase.

How do you keep them from buying online or at another store? One way is to have the product in stock. Another way is to add value. You can add value in several ways, from the attitude of employees to the vibe of the salon to your return policy. The expertise you and your staff demonstrate also adds value in that the client has someone to turn to for advice and troubleshooting.

Purchasing

In the purchasing phase, the decision has been made and the consumer acquires their desired product. It may seem obvious, but this is the moment where all the hard work of putting together tasteful displays, attractive and informative literature and a team of smart, dedicated employees comes together. The process of selling (which we'll touch on later) has paid off and you've made the sale.

Many think that purchasing is where the sales process ends; although it is the most important phase as it relates to your bottom line, it's not the end. What may be more important than the purchasing phase is the outcome of the assessment phase and its impact on return clients.

Assessment

Once the purchase is complete, your clients will have to live with their products. During this time, the product and the whole process of buying – from how the store looked to how the sale went – will undergo serious assessment. In the end, your client will decide one of three things: the product performs below their expectations, on par with their expectations or it exceeds their expectations. Their assessment of the product and the sales process will be major factors in determining whether they return for more services and products or not. For your bottom line, it's the difference between one $100 salon appointment and $50 sale or 20 of the same services from that return client.

How do you ensure the client is happy?

You can't, not always, but you can make the sales process easy. Not every client will love every product they purchase, but if you make the sales process fun and informative, and make the return process hassle-free, then their displeasure with the product will be overshadowed with their positive sales experience.

Likewise, if you sell a client a product or tool they love, use daily and share with their friends, but the sales experience is negative, they'll do three things: not come back, buy their product from a competitor and become an anti-evangelist for your salon. Trust us, you don't want any of this.

You can always develop a customer satisfaction survey to ask clients via email, phone or in person. Several online tools – like surveytool.com and surveymonkey.com – offer low-cost, anonymous surveys. Or you could develop your own.

Online Customer Satisfaction Survey Resources:

www.surveytool.com   www.questionpro.com

www.surveymonkey.com   www.zoomerang.com

THE PROS KNOW

"We have great products because we have a belief system in the salon – the staff believes in our products and so do our customers."

Jill Krahn
Hair Success Salons and Spas, Fargo, ND

Ensure your client's happiness by:

- **Selling high-quality products from reputable dealers** (if you wouldn't use it yourself or won't use it in your salon, why are you carrying it?)

- **Providing clients with enough information to make an educated decision based on the products you carry**

- **Giving clients support after the purchase.** This means being available for a quick tutorial on how to apply a product or use a tool, being willing and able to answer a question about the product or tool and having the knowledge to pass on the right information.

- **Make sure your products and tools deliver what they promise** (again, if you wouldn't use it, why sell it? There isn't much that's more convincing than an expert – that's you – saying they use and love a product).

- **Be up front with your return policy**

- **Reinforcing the good decision they made to purchase that particular product or tool**

Customer Satisfaction Survey Questions

- How satisfied are you with the services you purchased on [date]?
- How satisfied are you with the products you have purchased at [salon]?
- How satisfied are you with the customer service you received?
- How satisfied are you with [salon]?
- We strive to exceed your expectations, what could we have done to make your experience better?
- How likely are you to return for salon services in the future?
- Why?
- How likely are you to buy products from us in the future?
- Why?
- How likely are you to recommend [salon] to others?
- What would you like to let your stylist know about your visit?
- What additional services or products would you like to see at [salon]?

Check It Out: When Selling Retail to Your Clients, Remember:

- Your clients don't have to buy from you. Your education, professionalism and attitude will convince a shopper to buy from you or take their business elsewhere.

- People go to grocery stores for food and salons for hair products. Unfortunately, your clients can buy many hair products in both places. Your job is to give them the buying experience they're looking for and demonstrate the superiority of your salon product as compared to what's at the grocery store.

THE PROS KNOW

"Clients buy my retail because they believe in it. It's not always the price point that drives them to buy, sometimes getting them to use the product while in the chair gets them to realize the benefit of using it. Your stylist must be considered a hair expert and authority."

Sharon Barajas
Woody's Quality Grooming, Associate Marketing Manager

CHAPTER 19

Marketing Mindset: Sales Strategies

"People share, read and buy almost anything when the content or product is introduced through friends and people they know and trust."

—Malorie Lulich

For success in a retail salon, you have to think about your products strategically. You have to be able to see how the product, price, offer and display work together to make yours the most appealing salon to the customers you want.

Your Product P.O.D.

What's a pod? It's a self-contained capsule; in your salon, it's the zone. A pod is more than that; for your salon, it's the Price Offer Display system of retail sales. The POD concept can be applied to any zone in the salon, but we want to boost your retail sales and set you up for a long, lucrative business life, so we're looking only at the product POD.

As we said, success in retail depends on how the product relates to price, offer and display and there are really only four easy rules to remember.

Product POD Rules

Select the best *product* available. Not the most expensive, but the one that will fit your client's needs and pocketbook, as well as your salon's look and feel, best.

Price it fairly, but always with profit in mind.

Offer discounts, bundles, packages and other buying incentives.

Display your products in a neat, tasteful manner that invites people to look, feel, smell the product and that drives them to desire the product or what the product represents.

How do you price your product?

Retail pricing is a tricky thing. Price too high, no one buys and you lose money. Price too low and everyone buys and you lose money. Price just right, you move product and make money. So, how do you arrive at a price?

It's an easy formula: Cost of order + shipping / total number of pieces = true cost.

True cost x 2 = final price.

Take a look at this. You order 100 travel size shampoos at a cost of $200 + $20 shipping.

$200 + $20 = $220

You ordered 100 pieces: $220 / 100 = $2.20

Your true cost per good is $2.20 (price plus shipping).

To arrive at your retail price, multiply it by two: $2.20 x 2 = $4.40

That gives you a profit of $2.20 on each one sold.

Not all things are priced equally. For less expensive items, like the travel shampoo above, you may want to multiply your price by a factor of 2.5 (for a price of $5.50 and a $3.30 profit) or more. For more expensive items, like a salon-quality blow dryer ($220.00), you may want to multiply it by far less, like 1.25 (giving you a price of $275).

> **NOTE**
>
> Look around at other stores in your neighborhood. What are their prices like? Expensive? Average? Cheap? This will give you some insight into pricing your products and services.

As you can see, smaller items have a higher tolerance for higher markup and greater profit per piece. Again, if we look at a case of 1,000 tinted lip balms for $100 plus $15 shipping, we do: $200 + $15 / 1,000 = $0.215. At less than a quarter each for total cost of goods, your potential for profit is greatly increased. Multiply your cost by a factor of 10 and you have a price of $2.15 each and a profit of $1.93 per piece. Pull that out to your 1,000-piece order and you have a profit of $1,930.

Pricing does depend on the tolerance your clients. In an upscale neighborhood, a high price may signify a higher class, where in a middle-class neighborhood that same price may represent a lifestyle or cost that is just out of reach.

What do I Offer?

For real success in a retail salon, you can't rely on individual services and single-product sales, you have to offer product bundles, pampering packages, discounts on multiple services and specials throughout the year. Let's talk about some general product and service offers and move into season- and holiday-specific specials.

Product and service offers fall into several categories, which includes: buy one get one (BOGO), bundled discounts, price reductions, seasonal specials and group discounts.

- **BOGO:** Buy one, get one specials are always popular with consumers. They perceive a great savings and great discount, but if you look at how items are priced, you'll find both savings and profits built in.

  Take our lip balm selling for $2.15. If we sell them buy one, get one half off, we sell two for $3.22, but only have $0.42 tied up in the product.

  If you know you're going to offer a BOGO special, you can increase the price of the product, which raises your profits, only to discount it back to normal levels. Again, take our lip balm. If we want to offer 10% off all lip moisturizers but keep profits the same, raise the price of the product. A 15% increase in price, puts the lip balm at $2.47, only $.30 more per item. A 10% discount brings the product down to only $2.22, which is slightly above what your "normal" expected retail would be.

  If you're going to manipulate prices like this, we suggest that you do it from the start, otherwise you have clients complaining that you raised prices or weren't true to your guarantee of value. It's easier to start higher and reduce the price than it is to increase the price and maintain the same income level and sales volume.

  Another note on BOGO. BOGO sales take all sorts of shapes. BOGO half off. BOGO free. Buy two, get one free (or half off). Buy two, get three. You can limit the BOGO to the same product line, brand or price point (for a good example of how to do a BOGO special, look at your grocery store: chicken is BOGO free and you pay for the more expensive one). Your BOGO offers don't just have to be on retail, you can offer service packages as well – every fifth styling visit is free (or discounted), every sixth color gets free highlights (great offer because not everyone will take advantage of it). We'll get more into loyalty programs, which is where many of the service offers fall, a little later.

- **Bundled Discounts:** Offering packages of bundled products does more than increase sales one time, it introduces clients to new products and services they may not have known about or tried on their own and it gets them to return (and repeat customers are worth a lot more to your salon than one-time buyers).

  Bundle ideas include a men's grooming bundle (a selection of three: aftershave, shampoo, conditioner, moisturizer, shaving kit items, face wash and hair gel or something similar), shampoo and conditioner multiples (color-care shampoo, conditioner and leave-in conditioner; shampoo, conditioner, styling product bundles for specific hair types or colors), treatment bundles (manicure and pedicure discounts; multiple-area waxing discounts; cut, color, style packages; wedding or prom makeup, hair and waxing bundles).

  You get the idea. Take a close look at your clients and learn what they want, what lives they want to lead, what celebrities and trends they follow, what their interests are, then build your bundles around that. Who knows, maybe a sports treatment package (for runners: sports mani/pedi, and a post race sports massage and shampoo, cut and style), mommy-daughter day of pampering (adult and kid's cuts and styles, plus makeup). You know your clients. Offer them bundles and packages they can't refuse.

- **Pampering Packages:** Pampering packages are a little like bundles, but focus more on the luxury and relaxation side of the salon and spa, rather than the standard cut, color, style or retail side. Perfect examples would be girls' getaway packages, bachelorette parties, mother-daughter (of any age) packages, couples treatments and packages that reflect anything about the cultures, interests, desires and lifestyles of your clients.

  What do the packages include? Anything you want them to include. A massage, haircut, style and take-home product. A manicure, pedicure and facial. These packages can be anything, so long as they reflect your clients.

- **Multiple Services Discounts:** In some ways you could call this a "Build Your Own Bundle" program. Develop a menu of salon services and offer a discount on multiples. If you normally charge $25 each for a manicure, pedicure, brow waxing, lip waxing, 15-minute facial, 15-minute neck and shoulder massage, how about charging $80 for any four booked at the same time?

  If you think about the current trend in restaurants of doing a prix fixe (fixed price, pronounced prefix) menu, it's the same thing. For $25, each diner gets their choice of two appetizers, three entrées and two desserts. Develop your prix fixe salon menu. Appetizers: 10-minute neck or foot massage. Entrée: facial scrub, mani/pedi or blowout/styling. Dessert: aromatherapy, deep moisturizing, makeup application. How could you build your own salon prix fixe menu?

- **Seasonal Specials:** Seasonal and holiday specials are always big sellers. In addition to gift cards for services and gift packages of products (both of which you should have), special offers that reflect the season and holiday always sell well. Take a look at these ideas for specials throughout the year.

  1. **New Year, New You.** Just after new years, offer packages to clients that reflect upon the new year. Update their hairstyle with new, trendy, innovative cuts and styles, and support it with products and color treatments. Offer a relaxation package to get them started fresh.

  2. **Valentine's Day.** Sure, offer packages for her – cut and color, waxing, facial scrubs, et cetera – but focus on him. Deep discounts on men's haircuts (this draws in new male clients and gives a little something to the loyal male clients). Gift bags including masculine products, massage oils and aromatherapy candles or oils. We know that men are less likely to pamper themselves, so focus on selling his beauty to the women and significant others in his life. Signage like "He's your diamond in the rough, let us help make him shine" or "You fell in love with him for a reason, we'll show you why" or "Bring him in for an overhaul" is both cheeky and gets the point across that you're offering great men's salon packages.

  3. **Mother's Day.** Mother's Day specials should do two things: get moms in the door and send them home with products they'll love. Mother's Day specials should focus more on pampering mom, giving her a break from the day-to-day life of kids, work and household chores. Offer packages that include mini massages; nail treatments; easy (and profitable) hair treatments like shampoos and styling,

highlights, quick color treatments and trims or cuts; and waxing.

4. **Memorial Day.** We know what you're thinking: Memorial Day? Yes. It's the opening of summer and the perfect time to offer summer cuts and styles, skin-care products, tanning (spray, gel, tanning bed) treatments, pedicures (time for sandals, which means its time for cute toes).

5. **Summer Specials.** Like with Memorial Day specials, summer specials focus on skin care and sun protection, hair management (the sun is hard on hair, especially colored hair, offer treatments accordingly) and mani/pedi maintenance.

6. **Father's Day.** As with Mother's Day, Father's Day specials should center on treating dad. Sports massages, back waxes, shaves, brow treatments, skin treatments, even manicures give dad a little pampering he wouldn't have given himself.

7. **Labor Day.** Help clients recover from the harsh summer sun. The perfect bookend to your Memorial Day and Summer specials. Offer treatments and products that ensure healthy skin and hair, and a relaxing landing from the madness of summer. You could also offer packages that extend the summer season with tanning solutions and other products and treatments that support that summer vibe.

8. **Halloween.** Offer fun temporary colors and crazy styles (think of the Bride of Frankenstein or Marge Simpson or even a mullet) with a follow up treatment a day or two later to wash out the color, fix the style and get your client out of character and back into their life.

9. **Holidays.** Be careful not to run specials that would alienate your customer base. Christmas, Hanukkah, Eid and Tet specials all speak to one culture or religion, but we want the salon to draw in clients from all walks of life, so go with Holiday Specials. With your holiday specials, offer products (that can be given away as gifts) paired with treatments, special gift baskets, gift cards and introductory packages for your client's friends and family (and throw in a perk for them as well).

10. **Winter Blues.** An alternative to the New Year, New You special, offer a Winter Blues package designed to freshen up clients and drag them out of the midwinter doldrums that come after too many months of cold weather and early nights.

Tips

Use your specials as ways to get new clients in the door. Gift cards and gift packages that must be redeemed in your salon will bring in new clients. Then all you have to do is keep them (but that's easy, the products, salon and spa treatments and the customer service you provide is far better than your competitors).

How Do I Display It?

We've cover a lot of positive display options, but to recap, the rules are simple: clean, neat displays that allow the client to see, touch and smell the product; well lit; informational signage; show clients how the product gives them the lifestyle they desire.

THAT'S WHAT THEY SAY

You can have the greatest specials in the history of the world, but with an unmotivated staff, you'll never sell even one. How do Nikki Lee and Riawana Capri of Nine Zero One Salon in West Hollywood, Ca., provide motivation? By making it fun.

"In the past few quarters we've held product-selling contests among our stylists and staff; we turned a poster board into a game board with prizes and decorations to keep track of everyone's progress. Everyone on our team has responded because it brings an element of fun when getting clients to try products that will ultimately help them maintain their hair."

But what about negative options? With all these products and specials, it's easy to fall into some old and bad habits. Here are a few things to avoid.

1. **Don't put up a Christmas tree.** Department stores will put up bigger and better trees and yours will look second-rate. Plus, it speaks to the Holiday Special theory of cultural and religious alienation. Keep your decorations subtle – use bright colors (not the typical red and green) – and seasonally themed. A beautiful gift bag with a silver snowflake works well for many months, where a reindeer gift bag has a one-month shelf life.

2. **Don't use crazy props.** Avoid outrageous props like your typical holiday-themed cutouts – pumpkins, cats, Santa, a turkey – you don't want your salon to look like a second-grade classroom.

3. **Don't overcrowd your display.** Give your products the room they need to breathe and shine.

4. **Don't junk up your stations.** Salon and spa stations should be neat, organized and useful. The necessary tools should be within reach and the featured products easily accessible for the stylist to use and client to see.

5. **Keep the personal personal.** This one will be a tough sell, but keep the personal photos (of kids, dogs, vacations, et cetera) out of sight in the salon and spa area. Your employees aren't at work to show off their lives; they're there to improve the lives of the clients. Give employees a space of their own to show off pictures and mementos. Try a bulletin board by the shampoo station and label it with "Meet The [salon name] Family." Remember, not all of your clients are your friends, nor do they have to be. This is a business and it's ok to have business-only relationships.

> **NOTE**
>
> Your specials come in two varieties: product based and service based. In product-based specials you're offering products exclusively; in service-based, the focus is on salon and spa services. To maximize profit potential in all zones in your salon, **combine the two special packages and offer a product and service.** For example: a Mother's Day salon/spa package might include a mani/pedi, highlights and an aromatherapy candle; a BOGO sale might include a service as the primary purchase and a complimentary product as the "get one free" (or half off).

When Pricing Your Retail, Did You...

- Remember to add in shipping, advertising, shopping bags and costs of any promotions into the final price?

- Price the products too high and put them out of reach from most of your customers?

- Offer promotions or bundle two or more products together for a lower price?

- Remember to promote retail heavily during the holidays? Most people are in a good, buying mood during the holidays, give them something to celebrate in your store.

THE PROS KNOW

Chris Pearson of Mistic Hair in Tampa, FL, has two great pieces of advice:

"The distributor gives us the suggested retail price for the product. Let's say I buy it for $8, the suggested retail is $16. I add $1 for education and marketing. You would be surprised at how quickly it adds up. Using manufacturer recommended pricing usually doesn't price you out of the neighborhood."

"We use every inch of space. We defy the rule of no retail below the waist. Display some products at eye level with the seating area. We always keep inventory stock filled on the shelves because if they look empty, it looks like you're going out of business."

CHAPTER 20

Six Things That Drive Away Business

"As far as the customer is concerned, the interface is the product."

—Jef Raskin

Y ou work hard to bring new clients in the door and keep returning clients happy, but are you guilty of business operations that may actually push them away? Take a look at these five things that drive away business, then read on to see ways you can fix them.

1. Overly complicated telephone tree messaging systems.
2. Not returning calls and messages or confirming appointments.
3. Cluttered Web pages that are hard to navigate and slow to load.
4. Putting clients on group email lists without their permission.
5. Sending out too many promotional emails.
6. A traffic jam at the reception desk whether checking in or out.

They look simple, and they are, but clients find them annoying (and so do you, remember the last time you called a customer service line and got lost in the phone tree?) and they're easy to fix.

• Simplify your phone tree. Rather than schedule appointments with individual employees, schedule appointments by department (Press 1 for Salon, Press 2 for Manicure/Pedicure, Press 3 for the Spa…) and have the receptionist give a human touch for that final bit of scheduling.

• Better yet, eliminate the phone tree and have someone live answer the phone every time. Does that mean you don't use voicemail? No. It just means you use it much more simply: "You've reached Sol Salon, we're helping another client, but your call is important. If you leave your name, number and a brief message, we'll return your call as soon as possible".

- Return your calls. Keep a notepad by the phone so you can jot down phone numbers left in voicemails. As you call them back, cross them off. It's an easy habit to develop.

- Redesign your website. Graphics heavy, flash-enabled, music-laden Web pages are a thing of the past. Simplify the format to be cleaner and more elegant. No matter the style of your salon, a clean, easy to browse Web pages will fit your vibe.

- On Web pages, avoid flash if possible. Flash doesn't work with current-generation iPhones and iPads and you don't want your salon to be passed over by potential iPad-using clients (who will on average have more disposable income) because they couldn't load your site.

- Always ask for permission to email clients about specials, events and new products.

- Keep your emails to a reasonable number. Once a week is too much, but once a month is just right for a regular newsletter-style email with clients. Then break in once during the month to announce a special or product.

> *Tips*
>
> Treat your clients as you want to be treated and you'll create an excellent client experience in your salon.

THE PROS KNOW

"The main things that can kill retail are dusty shelves and dirty displays. If it's not clean, they aren't buying it. Have you ever bought three-day-old fish? No. Why would you expect your clients to do the same."

Chris Pearson
Mistic Hair, Tampa, Fl.

"Customers cannot wait to be waited on. That is the number one no-no for retail: no lines, no waiting. People want here and now service. People don't want to wait. People have lots to do and, if your service is slow, they'll take their business somewhere else."

Kristen Kole
Imperial Salons and Spa, Melbourne, Fl.

CHAPTER 21

Marketing and Sales Secrets

"People don't buy for logical reasons. They buy for emotional reasons."

—Zig Ziglar

What is it that makes all of us want to buy something we may or may not need. Some of us love to shop until we drop, others loath going into any store especially to buy products such as retail or body anti-aging products. Maybe it's because we just don't know enough about these types of products or we just think we can't afford it or may or not be necessary.

Retailers have come up with many ways to entice us into getting into the buying mode. I call them buying secrets. These little secrets enable them to get the hardest customer to stop, look and even touch retail that they may never have any desire to buy. Even the toughest customer deep down wants to make a purchase that may make them feel or look good even though they may not need it.

We have all stepped foot in a department store and had to navigate through the beauty and fragrance gauntlet. A beautiful woman in a lab coat immediately bombards you. She may spritz you with the newest fragrance or lotion with the intent of selling you a bottle of perfume or maybe talking you into a makeover guaranteeing you to look, smell and feel younger. It is difficult to walk away without being given a free sample.

I have stopped, taken a sample and sometimes purchased a bottle of perfume for my wife. Is it because the sales person is beautiful or handsome, well rehearsed, knowledgeable, educated in the product's he or she is trying to sell me? They must be experts because of how much confidence they portray, the medical lab coat he or she is wearing must mean they have some type of degree in the medical field, right? And how quickly they were to disparage the products my wife and I currently have been using.

Does all this make us feel obligated once we stop and step into the beautiful smelling, comfortable setting with soft music playing in the background, to make a purchase? Have you noticed the first thing they show you is the most expensive product? On the counter, there is a variety of much cheaper items. I call these the pocket stuffers, $20 and under. The I don't need any of these but I don't have to spend $100 and I can get away from this sales person purchase. How many of us have done this? I know I have. You don't feel as bad knowing you bought something because the sales person spent so much time with you. Mission accomplished!

The counters are clean and the glass display case is spotless with not a fingerprint to be found. This is not done by accident. Big retailers have strategized and used these techniques for years. They have spent billions getting to understand what makes us buy or not buy as consumers.

We will encourage you to put these buying tactics or as I call them "secrets" to work in your retail store environment. Listed below are several of the top and easy to follow best-kept secrets for your business.

Invoke science

The best thing you can do in your business is to establish a dress code for your sales people who will be selling products. Clinique came up with the best marketing idea ever created. They put their sales people in white lab coats. In today's world people are trained and respect what people have to say in white lab coats. A makeup or counter person in a white lab coat establisher's that he or she is an expert. Of course they must be well versed in the products they are selling but is a surefire way to sell beauty and retail products.

Play the expert – Play on the philosophy of the brands your selling. Explain in detail the long list of proven facts about your products and have a list of any of today's stars that may be using these brands. If they're using it, it must be good and should have the same results to your customers.

> **NOTE**
>
> With the introduction of added services such as shaves, color services, and pedicures, upgraded and larger hot water heaters are necessary in most barbershops and grooming salons. Remember to add this to your startup expense!

More expensive equal's better – Selling a product that is twice as much money as anything else must mean it is better than any other brand and symbolizes a certain status and of course reputation as being the best. The "if it's more expensive it must be better" mentality trick is one of the oldest in retailing, but still works today. Many of us are fighting the anti aging bug. If we spend more on a hair gel or makeup that cost more many of us think it will make us feel better and look younger also being able to make that purchase as we get older is also a way of saying that we have worked hard and we owe that much to ourselves. I call this the "feel good we earned it" purchase.

The Nose Knows

This is a clever trick, but many retailers today pump certain smells into the air to put you into the buying mode. Certain department stores rely on fragrance to help sell bathing suits by having a coconut, beach-like smell in that area. Infant apparel gets the baby powder smell and lingerie gets a lilac smell.

In a salon retail environment, lighting a few scented candles can give your salon or retail store the exact smell you are trying to set in your store. The more pleasurable you make the shopping experience, the more likely your customers are to stay longer and buy more. How many times have you found yourself buying something that smelled so good you had to have it? Music to your ears- Many retail stores play music to keep shoppers relaxed, giving them a soothing feeling which keeps them in a happy state. When a customer is happy they tend to splurge on things they may or may not need. If you're catering to a older clientele, it makes sense to play music from their era. This will bring them back to happier times and remind them of days in the past. If you cater to a younger generation, it makes sense to play music they listen to. You can always go with soft, soothing elevator music. This tends to work on all generations.

Make the Puzzle Fit

If you're a big retailer or a small mom and pop, make all the parts come together. If you're catering to makeup let your shoppers see how all the parts come together. Eyeliner, lipstick, and blush should all be in one section. You do not want then wondering around your store trying to figure out they should get ready for a night on the town. Make it simple, keep it close and make sure the price is right. Let the entire makeover fit in their budget don't let them leave without having everything they need in hands reach to do what is necessary for their makeover.

It also makes sense to have a mannequin dressed from head to toe, dripping in accessories. The more they see how the end result will look when they are finished the more they will spend. Buyers like to see what they may look like by imagining themselves in what you have on display or on your shelves.

Make it Shine

What do new cars and diamonds have in common? They're both shiny and they're both expensive. Those things are not coincidental, and retailers know it. It's almost a physical response. Humans automatically assume something that gleams is fancy and valuable. If you want to be successful in retail, your counters and every surface that products rest on must gleam and shine. Give the customer the impression your products are worth every penny your selling them for.

Door Buster

We all want a bargain. Big retailers have had door buster days for years. The morning after Thanksgiving has been a retailers dream for as far back as I can remember. Why is it that the customer is compelled to rush to the store to buy the same thing he could have the day before that may not be rare or even valuable?? The art of shopping itself, the high of knowing they get from being there is why they come in the first place. And stores take advantage by turning it into an adrenaline charged event.

Your business can also offer these one-day sales or door busters. Let your customer know that you are planning an event, tell them you will be dropping prices on special items. Email them, call them, send a postcard, post it, text it, make it an extravaganza. There is no reason your event cant give the customers the same adrenaline rush the big stores do with the same type of results.

✓ CHECK IT OUT

Little secrets that you must never pass onto your competitors-

- Remember to play soothing music at all times
- Light a scented candle or spray your work environment with beautifully scented musk or perfume
- Keep your counters and shelves shining and clean
- Have a dress code for your sales team
- Remember to make the puzzle fit

Don't forget about your employees, they're your sales force and your biggest tool in converting styling customers into loyal retail buyers. Your employees will need training (which is often available through vendors or outside agencies like a small business group) and a fair commission. But how do you structure a commission?

There are two basic ways: flat commission and tiered commission. In a flat commission, you pay between 10% and 20% of total retail sales back to the sales person (most often the stylist in your salon); some salons pay this out monthly, quarterly or annually.

Tiered commissions pay a higher percentage for a higher volume. For instance, on sales from $1-$100, 10%; $101-$250, 15%; $251-$500, 20%; $501 and up, 25%. Your sales goals and percentages will vary based on how often you pay (the example above is for one month of retail sales, on a quarterly pay scale, the highest end starts at $1,501; on annual payouts, the high end starts at $6,001).

Some salon owners get creative with their use of sales commissions. Rather than pay out the full amount, they'll make partial payments to the stylists and staff, while they put the rest of it back for a yearly retreat. Imagine stealing away for an all-expenses-paid (by your hard work in sales) beach house weekend with your stylists. How would that improve morale? By diverting a portion of the sales commissions into that pool of money, salon-wide rewards become a real possibility.

Tips

Ask around for how other salons (or jewelry stores or other business that work on a commission basis) structure their sales commissions. Fix your commissions to be fair and competitive with other salons, but still profitable for you and worthwhile for your staff.

Recommendation from the Pros

Jill Krahn of The Salon Professional Academy shared some of her sales secrets with us. Here are seven things she says a successful retail salon needs to know:

1. **Make sure the staff is fully trained in the products you carry.**

2. **Create an incentive for sales. Offer them something realistic, attainable and desired - cash, a day off with pay or dinner out always work.**

3. **Set up weekly goals for the staff and follow up with them to ensure they're meeting these goals. If they aren't, see how you can help.**

4. **Regularly send out email blasts to your clients to announce sales, specials and new product arrivals.**

5. **As far as displays go, placement is the key. You need front window displays, counter displays and plenty of product that will ensure an effective showing of the product. And make sure all displays appear FULL at all times.**

6. **Get creative with your sales. Play "Deal or No Deal," or place colored dots on the bottom of candy kisses - each dot represents a different percentage off (or even free products or services).**

7. **Script your sales process so that everyone knows how to sell and how to represent the products you carry.**

THE PROS KNOW

"If a guest feels good after a service, their emotions will guide them to buy products. If they look good, they feel good and they buy products! Emotion wins!"

Kristen Kole
Imperial Salons and Spas, Melbourne, FL

CHAPTER 22

Retail Sales and the Male Client

*"I have never worked a day in my life without selling. If I
believe something, I sell it, and sell it hard."*

—Este Lauder

There's the old fashioned thought that barbershops are for men and salons are for women.
We've come a long way in crossing that line and now we have husbands, sons, boyfriends,
singles and men of all sorts visiting salons for cuts, styles, color treatments and even waxes.
You'd never restrict you salon services to miss out on the profit potential brought in by male
clients, but are you doing it with your retail?

It's true that women consume more of the beauty products available, but leaving your
male clientele out of the picture is like leaving money on the table. You don't have to carry
a lot of products for men, but a rack will do. Think of the products men want – shave gels
and creams, shampoo, styling products, aftershave – and the tools – razors, beard and body
trimmers, other personal grooming tools – and carry a selection for them.

Selling retail products to male clients is not as hard as you think, but it does require a little
effort applied consistently when they sit in the styling chair. We spoke with Gino Stampora
from Stampora Consulting about selling to male clients; here's what he had to say:

How to Sell Retail to Male Clients

Why does it seem so hard to sell retail products to male clients? Any customer requires
different techniques and methods of selling to close a retail sale. Men shop differently than
woman but don't exclude them when trying to sell retail. Men do buy! We have to look at the
different techniques that have had success and use them to help close retail sales.

It amazes me how many times I have heard stylists and barbers say that they do not have
much luck selling to their male client base. Many have given up and barely bring up retail at
all. Why is it that you can sell to your female customers? Have you thought about your sales
techniques? Knowing the difference in the sales approach is key to be successful in retailing
to men.

Understand this about your male customers:

- Men are not price driven. We may say yes, but deep down we are like a boy discovering your merchandise for the first time.

- We tend to spend more on products if we are made to feel it will make us look younger, better looking and attractive to the opposite sex. If you can make us believe that your product will do this, we will buy it.

- We often show how much we love a person we are buying for by the price tag of the gift we choose. The more expensive, the more it means we love the person.

- When we do buy for ourselves, it is a viewed as a special treat. We often spend so much of our money on family that it is rare that we spend on ourselves. Don't try to limit us if we do feel the need to buy.

- Above all most men don't have the time to shop, most view it as a chore. Keeping this in mind when your cutting and styling you should be selling.

- If you can make the grey go away, make our hair look fuller and richer. You will have a steady retail customer but if it doesn't work we will not be back for seconds.

- Don't forget, men buy for the women, or men, in their lives, so a gift for a loved on is always a selling point.

Tips

Men don't traditionally shop for hair products, so you have to lead them to the products you think would serve their needs best. Having products at the checkout is key — they, like everyone else, get sucked in to buying and the last minute.

New Male Customers Become Repeat Customers

It is a fact that you can grow your business faster if you sell more retail products to the same customers. You have already invested in finding the customer and they may be a regular, but to grow business they must buy retail. Wouldn't it be great if you could get every one of your male clients to buy retail? Your average ticket in the salon or barbershop would grow significantly. You can achieve this with some thought and planning and basic understanding of each of your male clients. You do not have to be a hard core salesperson, but it does require a little effort, applied consistently. Follow these five steps to better retail sales to your male clients.

Tips

Men want to see and touch products, so let them use products in the chair.

1) **Consult your client** – During the service you are providing for your male client, ask them, "What don't you like about your hair?" "Do you feel old with your current style" "Are you happy with your hair color?" Please remember doing this after the haircut is not the time. Most men are on the go. If you are hoping for a sale when your client is paying the bill, you will most likely not get a retail sale. Explaining the benefits of your products and actually showing them how they work and smell and feel while cutting and styling will almost guarantee that your male client will buy your retail products. Don't be afraid to put some to their hand, let them feel it, touch and show them how to apply it to themselves.

Know your product and don't hesitate in offering it to him. How much confidence you have in the product will enable you to better explain the product and the advantages in using it. Men are more likely to buy from someone who truly understands and is educated and believes in the retail products they sell.

2) **Hand him the bottle** – Handing the bottle to the client gives him a sense of ownership in the product and allows him to open the top, smell it and read the label, making him more comfortable with it. Remember to make sure the bottles are impeccably clean and never hand a client a crusty, dusty bottle of gel. Men see dust, they immediately think old and out of style.

3) **Show them how to use it** – Men buy things on impulse, most don't read directions and if you sell them something and they are not using it right they will immediately stop using it and never buy it again. The biggest complaint men have after leaving a salon or barber shop is that when they tried the product at home it did not work. Why? Because you as the retail expert, stylist or barber did not give them the step by step instructions on how to apply the retail products when they get home. Whenever possible, get them involved and let them play with the product. Even if it means you have to rinse their hair and apply the product again. Men must be confident that they will be correctly using the product at home or he will never buy it again.

4) **Ask for the sale** – He won't buy it if you don't ask. Most men will never bring up retail products. If you don't bring it up shame on you. He won't buy it unless you ask, but make sure you compliment when you do. There is nothing better than your stylist or barber saying you look younger, cool, and handsome when you leave their place of business. So, ask for the sale before they get out of your chair!

5) **Guarantee it** – Don't be afraid to say, "I personally guarantee you will be happy with this product. If you are not, bring it back and I will exchange it or give you a refund." Wow, what a powerful statement. This will make anyone feel more comfortable when buying a retail product. In today's world, the flexibility to return something you may not be happy with especially after using it is unheard of. This should make your male client a retail buyer for life.

Why Selling Retail to Men is so Important to Your Business

In today's world, it is so important to maintain our current customer base at the same time increasing daily sales. Retail is a big part of running a successful business and allows us to increase the actual size of a sale for every customer that walks through the front door of your place of business.

The success of your retail store, beauty salon or barber shop will be based on how much you emphasize product sales. Lets look at several reasons that retailing to men and how it gives you as a business owner a golden opportunity.

Tips

Men are loyal clients. Once they walk out the door and get one compliment, they are yours for life. That one compliment keeps them buying from you forever.

Retail products keep you on his mind – When your male client picks up a bottle of shampoo, gel or styling paste at home, he thinks of where he got it and who sold it to him. That bottle is a daily reminder of the great service he received and also the next haircut, color or shave he may need. A good male client comes in about every three weeks. Most woman four to six weeks. Overall if you can convert the male client into a retail buyer they often become more loyal them woman. Did I forget to say they are better tippers?

Products keep him coming back – Studies show that if a client buys a product, there is over a 90% chance that they will return to the shop where he made the purchase! Men will not shop around town to other retail stores, hair salons or barber shops to find the retail products they are using.

Products enhance your professional image – If, through the use of a retail product you sell can correct a problem a male client is having or enhance a look, you will have a client for life. Men respect knowledge and someone who can fix a problem that they may have had difficulty with.

Retailing to men or woman is really about knowing your customer. People men or woman will feel more comfortable buying a retail product from someone they know and respect and most of all trust. If you have a steady male customer believe me he is confident in you and most likely will buy retail from you if you follow the guidelines above you should have no problems growing your retail male client base.

Do You Know How to Treat Men When Selling Them Retail?

- Don't leave us alone we will run out of the store

- Don't follow us around or you will spook us (check in every few minutes)

- Acknowledge your return policies up front

- Take us by the hand if we never bought this type of product before

- If we can't decide on a couple of items, make it simple and narrow it down. Too much too quick and we walk - we like it simple

- If we are buying retail for our wife or friend, don't make it a big deal if we don't know what products she uses. Insult us and we're gone

- Educate us but don't make us seem like we are stupid. Most likely we have never used any retail products you are selling

- Educate us as much as you can

- Men love to touch, squeeze, smell and make a mess. Let us touch and feel the product

- Bring up products every time we sit in your chair. When you hit someone with a brick every time you see them, eventually they'll get what you're telling them

THE PROS KNOW

"Men have to trust their stylist, once they trust, they will buy. If you say 'This is exactly what you need,' they will take the stylist's recommendations. I also find that if you get to the wife of a male customer, their influence will encourage them to buy."

Maria Arias
Nolan Vincent Salons, Davie, FL

CHAPTER 23

Communicating with Your Customer

*"The art of communication, whether a handshake, hug, phone
call, email or text with your customers, is essential to your
business success."*

—Jeff Grissler

You are in large part responsible for your guests' image and self-esteem. For many women, their stylists are more than just beauty experts. They are also sounding boards, relationship advisers, and life-coaches. So how can you leverage this close relationship to help you build and maintain your retail business?

You'll learn the importance of branding and how to make sure your brand is representing your business positively. We'll discuss various types of communication and the best practices for each and the importance of knowing your guest's preference.

Branding Your Salon

Your brand image is the cornerstone of your reputation. Your brand consists of color scheme, image, graphics, and logo. Think about your favorite brands, what feelings and memories come to you when you see their image and logo in marketing materials? You want to create a "brand" that your guests associate with the feelings they have while they are in your salon. If your salon is a relaxing salon and day spa then you want your brand to reflect calm and relaxation but if your salon is high energy then your brand should reflect that feeling.

Your brand should be consistent across all mediums: the signs in your window, the color of your walls, the background of your website, your menu, your Facebook page, your Google Places listing, etc. Brand awareness is what you get when someone has a (hopefully positive) emotional reaction or memory when they see your image. When your guest gets an email from you, they should be transported to the feeling they get when they are in the salon to visit you. Consistency and repetition are the keys. Your goal is to be top of mind for your guests whenever possible and having your brand associated with each communication you send will help you do it.

How to Communicate

Choose how you are going to communicate with your guests and then try to be consistent. You must communicate with your customers when they are not in the salon in order to keep your brand top of mind so that next time they are in need of a service they will think of your salon. You can choose to communicate with your guests with thank you notes sent through the mail but may find that stamps and the amount of time it takes to prepare these types of communications are too costly both in time and money. Phone calls are another option that can be less expensive but more labor intensive and potentially more intrusive to the guest. You will probably find that you get mostly voice mails when using this method of communication and may not get the response you are looking for. Electronic communications are a more efficient way of getting in touch with your guests. With over 80% of adult Americans having email addresses, you may find that your guests prefer electronic communications.

Getting to know your customer

You must collect contact information from your guests in order to communicate with them electronically. The way in which you collect your customer's contact information will make all the difference in their willingness to give it. One method is via an intake form. Your guests will be familiar with this process because they do it at other businesses. On the form you will want to collect first and last name, telephone number, and email address. Some clients might be skeptical to give you this information, so I also suggest that on the form you tell them what you plan to do with their information. Setting expectations upfront is always a good idea and collecting information is no different. It could read something like this,

"This Salon provides (will one day provide) online communication for your convenience. You may choose to receive your confirmations via email or text message, requests appointments online, refer your friends via email, submit satisfaction surveys and receive special offers. We will never share or sell your information to any other party."

Your front desk staff needs to make this data collection a routine part of operations as quickly as possible, and they must understand that getting this information is critical to the long term success of the salon.

When to Communicate

To Confirm Appointments

You should consider providing your guests the ability to confirm visits with you via email or text message. Often they would prefer the less intrusive form of an email or text than a phone call. Electronic communications will cut down time that your front desk staff spends on the phone allowing your staff to focus more on educating and selling retail products to guests, pre-booking follow up appointments, and ensuring guest satisfaction. Spending less time making confirmation calls can help you turn the front desk cost-center into a guest services profit-center.

Communication for Retention

Retention of new and existing clients is one of the biggest indicators of the success of your salon. Focusing on repeat business from guests should be high on your priority list when it comes to customer communication. Here are three key communication strategies that can help you retain your guests.

1. Say Thank you

Your main goal with this communication is to make sure that your guests feel comfortable and welcomed back. Thank you communications should be sent within 24-48 hours after your guest has been in the salon. Your guest should feel appreciated for choosing your salon over any other. You can do this automatically via email and software programs designed for this function, or you can go the old fashioned route of a hand written note, which can be a nice touch for first time guests. Your thank you letter should include appreciation for their last visit, information on how to contact you again should they wish to schedule another appointment, information about other services offered in the salon that they might want to take advantage of, and the details of your referral program. The most important element of a thank-you message is a survey. Especially as you get started, you must be consistently asking guests how you can improve.

2. Surveys

Surveying your repeat and new guests should always be a part of your retention strategy whether you've been open two months or 20 years. By asking key questions, you can help to ensure quality of service and you can use the feedback as a coaching tool for your team.

Example survey questions:

Were you greeted in a friendly manner?

Were all services performed to your satisfaction?

How would you rate your service provider?

How would you rate overall cleanliness?

Do you prefer online confirmations to phone calls?

Would you return? (Helps measure retention)

Would you refer a friend? (Helps to attract new guests)

Have you used any products recommend to you by your stylist? What was your experience using them?

Have you tried the products you purchased?

How well were you pleased with them?

3. Beauty Reminders

Pre-booking should always be one of your top goals in the salon, but no matter what you offer or how hard you try, you'll never be at a 100%. You will always have guests who will opt not to pre-book and for those clients I suggest beauty reminders. This would be a gentle reminder via email, text, post card or phone call that they have not been to see you in a while and would give them an easy way to request their next appointment. Sending these types of reminders is helpful for the client and can help you increase your frequency of visit if timed properly.

Marketing Your Salon Online

Search Engines

Google is the number one search engine in the world. It is important that you manage your listing on Google Places as this is often the first impression that a potential guest has of your business: to do this, simply go to http://www.google.com/places/ and claim your listing, by simply clicking on 'business owner?' at the top right of the page and following the instructions. Once you have followed the steps, you will be able to add photos (your logo for brand awareness and a picture of the outside of your salon to help clients with navigation from mobile devices!), list your specialties and the products you represent, and comment back to any reviews that are written about you.

People are going to write reviews about your business, it's up to you to manage your reputation. You can do this by responding to those reviews online. If the review is positive, thank them for it. If the review is negative, apologize and offer to make it up to them. This will show the online world that you are a conscientious business owner.

Other sites to consider checking on and claiming are Citysearch.com, Bing.com/local, yp.com, dexknows.com, local.yahoo.com, yelp.com, and foursquare.

Facebook

Social media marketing is a must-do for the future of your business. Facebook is the second most visited website in the United States. The salon industry has a unique opportunity to thrive through social media due to the closeness of the guest with her salon and her consumption of beauty related retail items. Each of your clients who connects with you on Facebook is also connected to an average of 150 other people who are likely to be in the same region and similar demographic. Use "viral marketing" to its fullest advantage. Viral marketing is using an existing social network (Facebook) to help promote your brand. In your case, you want your customers to "like," share," or "comment"

on posts that you make on Facebook because doing so will create buzz within their social network about you.

Here are a few steps:

1. Encourage each of your guests to check in to Facebook when they arrive at the salon. You can encourage this by doing token giveaways like complimentary samples if they check-in. Checking-in alerts their friends to which businesses and sites they visit, which gets your name brand out to more people similar to your client.

2. Ask your guests to "like" you on Facebook. Give them a good reason like periodic specials or last minute specials.

3. Try to post to your wall once per day. Consider what types of articles or posts your clients would be most likely to comment on or share with another of their friends.

While it's important to have as many followers as you can, the more important metric is to know how many people are talking about you on Facebook. The more people are talking about you, the more likely they are to click onto your page. Once you get them on your page you'll want to give them an action item; to request an appointment by giving them a phone number to call or a web form to fill out. All this Facebooking is for nothing if we aren't getting people in the chair!

Foursquare

Foursquare is an online and mobile based service that lets people announce to the world (and review for the world to see) places they go. Restaurants, bars, offices, museums, salons, stores and every other place you can think of are listed on Foursquare. Users "check in" to places and earn virtual badges (like "Mayor" for the person who visits most) for checking in. It's a fun, hip way to reach out to a youthful audience and even market specific offers to them.

> **NOTE**
>
> **Four types of successful Facebook posts:**
>
> **1. To show your personality.** Try pictures of the team, before & after pictures, any community events you participate in, wedding/baby announcements, etc.
>
> **2. To educate or inform.** Share an article about how to manage dry hair in the winter, fashion week pictures, product information or product sales.
>
> **3. To engage.** Ask a question or encourage comments. Ask for an opinion on new color or style, which new nail color they like best.
>
> **4. Just ask for what you want.** "Like, Share or Comment on this picture (of xyz product) by 2 p.m. to be entered for a drawing to win a full sized bottle!" I've seen easily 40-50 likes in a several hour window from posts like these; they really have a tendency to go viral.

Yelp

Yelp.com is the fastest growing online guide that helps people identify businesses and things around them. Shoppers look for trendy boutiques, diners look for the best restaurants and, if someone needs a salon, they can find yours if you're listed. Yelp incorporates user ratings and comments on your business, as well as a link to your website, email, twitter and phone number. Once you're listed on Yelp, ask your best customers to go on and give you a great review. You've given them a great haircut, they should be eager to return the favor.

Who used Yelp? Almost everyone. A wide range of users log in daily to search for places to shop, dine and visit. Most of all, the users of sites like Yelp are hip, and know what's happening in their city.

To invest in the future of your salon, you must invest in communicating to your customers. If you become the beauty expert for your client, connect with them in the way that is most convenient and meaningful for them, provide great service, and listen to their feedback they will make you a regular part of their lives for many years to come.

These simple steps below will help you consistently target your customer base.

- Salon Branding – Keep a consistent logo and color scheme across all marketing materials
- Make collecting customer contact information a habit
- Decide how you want to communicate with your guests and then be consistent
- Communicate to confirm, to thank, and to remind
- Manage your online reputation through Google, Facebook, Foursquare and Yelp

THE PROS KNOW

"The art of communicating with the customer is key. We wow the customer with a 15-minute consultation on their first visit. Every client gets a shorter consult on each visit so we can discover their hair needs and give them the best service possible."

Chris Pearson
Mistic Hair, Tampa, FL

"Good communication starts at 'Hi, welcome to our salon,' when the client walks in the door. Consultation is key to retailing. My team sells based on what the guest is requesting. You must listen in order to recommend the best product."

Kristen Kohl
Imperial Salons and Spas, Melbourne, FL

CHAPTER 24

Loyalty Programs

"The foundation stones for a balanced success are honesty,
character, integrity, faith, love and, most important, loyalty."

—Zig Ziglar

Satisfied and loyal customers are integral to your retail salon's success and longevity, but who are these customers? What sets them apart? How can you convert a one-time customer into a repeat client and then into someone who is loyal to your salon above all others? This chapter will give you some of the tools you need to keep clients happy, keep them returning and develop the loyal relationship you (and they) want.

Satisfied and Loyal Customers Explained

Satisfied Customers	Loyal Customers
May have been a client, but haven't developed a personal relationship with you or your salon.	Are repeat customers who use your product and service regularly and have built a relationship with you, their stylist (or technician) and your salon.
Have had little to no personal interactions with you or your salon.	Is a "brand evangelist" who tells everyone they meet about your salon and brings in new clients.
Will continue to do business with you until something better comes their way.	Know you, your salon and your employees, and will forgive minor faults (running late, et cetera) because they enjoy giving you their business.
View doing business with you as an act of convenience – your price is acceptable, location is ok and products suffice – but aren't excited about giving you their business.	Don't switch to a competitor because of perks or a "better" offer. They stay true to the relationships they've built.

To turn satisfied customers – who, frankly, find your service, salon and products acceptable at best and will leave at the first opportunity – into loyal customers – whose repeat business and brand evangelism will draw in friends and family and expand your client base quickly and steadily – doesn't take magic, it's just a matter of treating them right. That means exceptional customer service; friendly communication on the phone, in person or via email; and an incentive to return to your salon for their beauty needs.

That's where loyalty programs come in.

We all have that key ring filled with plastic tags from the grocery store, pharmacy, sporting goods shop and the 100 other places we shop. We also all have that stack of punch cards for free candles, cupcakes, lunches and ice cream. The reason we gather all of these rewards programs up and keep using them every time we patronize their respective businesses is simple – we want to get something for nothing.

Your retail distributor or manufacturer will supply you with:
- Marketing material
- Product reference guides
- Posters
- Shelf talker sets
- Loyalty program ideas

Buy 10 ice creams, get one free. 10 lunches and the 11th is on us. Five oil changes earn you a free car wash. We all know the offers and we give our favorites our business, but we know, as business owners, that nothing is ever free. The profit from selling you 10 ice creams is 30x that of the free one you'll get. Same with lunch. Same with the car wash. But we, as consumers, love it just the same.

Why wouldn't something similar work for you salon?

Getting Started

The saying goes that 20% of your customers provide 80% of your business. That 20% represents your top clients. Getting them, along with other current clients, to buy into your loyalty plan is smart business. That's why you start your loyalty program to reward current customers rather than draw in new ones. Any new ones you bring in are a bonus.

Start thinking about your loyalty program by jotting down some ideas. What services do you offer that are popular among your top clients? What are your best selling products? How frequently do clients buy a particular service or product? Is there a product or service you want to introduce to you clients, then to a larger audience? Are the things you're thinking of high profit or low profit?

What stands out to you as a good opportunity?

Next, look at how it would work. Is it a "buy X get one free" program? One that rewards clients for a total dollar amount spent? Does it involve a punch card, some computer tracking or some other way of keeping up with how close clients are to their reward? Is it time sensitive?

You know your salon, services, products and clients better than we do, so we know your ideas are solid. Take a look at a few loyalty program ideas we came up with.

Executing You Plan

Once you've settled on your loyalty program, it's time to execute, and that means keeping track of client spending and rewards. Don't worry, it can be easier than it sounds.

Example Loyalty Programs

1. **Referral Rewards Card.** Keep track of referrals who come in to your salon for treatments. For each new client, give the existing client a discount on a product or service. If they bring in five, give them a free treatment, service or product package. These can be actual cards (like business cards, which can be gotten for free or very cheaply from sites like vistaprint.com) with the existing client's name on there. When the new client presents it, they get 10% off their first service just for coming in.

2. **Frequent Service Rewards.** For clients who repeatedly get the same services – be it a haircut, color treatment, manicure, pedicure, massage, whatever – reward them for their frequency. Six color treatments and the seventh is on us – that rewards them for buying a higher-end treatment but keeps it profitable for you (you'd be giving away less than one treatment a year for clients who took advantage).

3. **Spending Rewards.** Spend a set amount on services or products and receive $25 in free products or services. When clients hit certain spending benchmarks – say, $500, $1,000, $1,500 in total spending – they receive a reward in line with their spending - $25, $50, $75 and so on. Set the spending benchmark according to your salon's pricing (maybe $250 is better than $500 for the first level, or maybe you want it to be $600 or $750 or some other amount) and keep the reward in balance with the benchmark. Rewards could also be in the form of free products, services or treatments, not just a $25 credit good toward anything.

4. **Product- or Service-specific Rewards.** Similar to the spending rewards, but focused on the products or services you want to sell. This is a great way to reward clients for repeat purchases of higher-end goods and services and can incentivize them to splurge on the higher-priced treatment more frequently in order to earn that reward.

5. **Discount Club Card.** This type of loyalty program gives clients instant rewards in the form of a percentage or dollar amount off each purchase. Sometimes businesses (like Sam's Club, BJ's and Costco) charge a membership fee for the privilege to buy their products at a discount, other times the discounts are small and the cards are free. You'll have to see what your market would tolerate, but either program – free-to-join or paid – can help increase sales.

   One way to offset any fee for joining is by making an initial offer with membership or renewal. If a client pays $25 a year for membership to the club, then offer a gift basket of sample size products (a low-cost way to introduce them to high-priced, high-profit items) or a discounted treatment.

One way to track spending and rewards is with a punch or stamp card. These cards are essentially business cards with spaces designated for stamps, initials or hole punches. The problem many of us encounter with these is that we lose them, forget to use them and somehow end up with a pile of cards, each with three things marked. An easy way around that is to keep a Rolodex beside the cash register. In the Rolodex, keep each client's rewards card. When they finalize their purchase, simply grab their card and register their purchase on it. This does several things for you: makes you know the clients by name (since you'll ask them every time for their name, soon you learn it), gives them peace of mind about the reward (they won't lose the card and the purchases, they know they'll get the reward) and it makes them talk about your salon, and your program, in a positive way.

VistaPrint.com offers low cost (even free) business cards of your own design. With a little work, you could put out your own inexpensive loyalty stamp/punch card.

Another way to track purchases is to utilize your computer software. Many Point of Sale systems (POS) will function as a cash register, invoicing system, inventory tracker and client data center. Tie your client's spending to a rewards benchmark and it will come up every time they check out. This may be more difficult or more expensive to do depending on your POS software; check with your sales representative or support staff for specifics.

Keep Them Coming Back For More

The main thing loyalty programs do is keep clients coming back for more. But with all the program options out there how do you know if your program is successful? One way is by analyzing the data through what's called A/B Testing.

A/B Testing works like this. Develop two rewards programs with two slightly different offers (a free to join 5% discount club and a $25/year 10% discount club). Make the offer to two groups of a similar size (only allow 10-20 clients in each). Then let it work. Track the spending and see which group uses their program more. Look at the habits for each group – what products/services do they buy? Are they within an acceptable margin? Has their spending increased or decreased? How frequently do they visit and use the program? After six months (it could be more or less depending on your salon), you should have enough data to fully develop the best plan.

Pick a distributor or manufacturer that offers:

- Social media tips and consultation
- An artists' network
- Rewards programs (for you and your clients)
- Business resources
- Artists' resources
- Education
- A business toolbox
- Public relations templates and online advertising assistance

CHAPTER 25

Promotions

*"Business is never so healthy as when, like a chicken, it must do
a certain amount of scratching around for what it gets."*

—Henry Ford

Promotions are another large piece to the retail puzzle. Promotions include everything from advertising to sales and specials. In this chapter, we'll give you some strategies that work and some ideas to think about when promoting your products, services, salon and people.

What are Promotions?

Simply put, promotions are things that get the word out about your salon and the products and services you provide. If you think of promotions as having three large parts – advertising, public relations and sales – it becomes easier to understand.

Advertising

You'll need to advertise, there's no way around it; but the frequency of your ads, the medium (print, radio, Internet or TV) and the message will all depend on your competition, your area and your desired customer. But what do you advertise?

Among other things:

- Advertise your store opening (essential to getting your name out)
- Advertise new services
- Advertise new products (especially if you have the exclusive on it)
- Advertise sales and specials
- Advertise major (positive) changes (new location, expanding the salon, adding a spa)
- Advertise new service providers when they join the salon

Successful ads all include the same basic parts: interesting and attractive visuals, an interesting line or two about the product/place/service, a call to action (where you tell the prospective client what to do – buy now, stop in today, try the product) and your contact information. As simple as it sounds, unless you have experience with advertising and are a good writer and designer, you'll need some professional help. Often magazines and newspapers can provide those services for you or can connect you with people who know their stuff.

There are four major components of every ad:

1. **Attract** the **Attention** of your prospective client
2. **Interest** them in the product or service
3. Cause them to **Desire** the product or service
4. **Demand Action** from them to buy the product or get the service

For your ad to be effective, it needs to be placed in publications (or on radio/TV shows or on websites) read, viewed and visited by your desired client. An easy place to start is with local magazines. A hip, punk-rock type salon may want to advertise in the free alternative weekly where it will be seen alongside the concerts, bar reviews and odd stories their ideal clients would read. But an upscale salon may benefit from advertising in a more exclusive publication that includes fashion stories, pieces about successful women in the community and luxury lifestyle. The average salon can find ways to fit in with both of these worlds, just be sure to do your homework on a publication or program before you commit to anything financially.

Public Relations

Public Relations, or PR, efforts can land you in the magazines and newspapers, and on the radio stations, TV shows, websites and blogs you want, without buying a traditional ad. PR works like this: you (or someone doing PR on your behalf) reach out to a reporter or editor at a publication and tell them what's going on in your salon, why it's interesting and, above all else, why it's news worthy of their printing. Success rates here are sometimes low, but a real story by a real reporter can do a lot more for your business than traditional advertising.

Hire It Out

If you've never done it, designing and writing an ad can be challenging. We recommend identifying a small marketing agency with retail (and preferably salon/spa) experience to develop an ad or series of ads for you. (If you can't find an agency that fits your goals and budget, try finding a graphic designer and writer team who can often create an ad at a lower cost than a traditional agency.) Different agencies will have different levels of experience with TV, radio, print and Internet ads, so make sure they are familiar with the different approaches you want to use.

Some story ideas for a PR push include:

1. The salon is opening and will bring new techniques/products/services
2. The salon hired a new employee
3. The salon organized a charity event (Locks of Love and similar)
4. The salon team participated in a charity event
5. The new product/service offered by your salon will add something entirely new to the area

PR, like advertising, is tricky. There's a formula and a protocol to getting the word out through a press release and it's a good idea to having a professional help. You can do an Internet search for "press release template" or "press release format," or hire a local publicist to create a release for you. On occasion, Small Business Administration groups will hold classes and seminars helping with PR efforts and we recommend attending one or more if you can.

One effective way to get some free publicity (well, not totally free, you may have time and products involved in this one) is to participate in fashion shows, charity fashion shows and model styling for local magazines. Get in contact with the editor and art director at a local women's or parents' magazine and see if your salon can help style models for photo shoots, or better yet, partner with a local boutique and magazine to offer a makeover and photo shoot for a reader. Any time you work with magazines, you'll get credit for hair and makeup (or whatever you provide), and when you work with fashion and runway shows, you'll get credit on the event program. All those times your name is in print is one more exposure to potential clients.

Sales

Sales always play a part in your advertising and PR efforts. After all, both an ad and an article are designed to do one thing – bring a new client into the store and drive them to purchase a product or service. Sales and specials on products and services support your call to action and send the prospect into your salon seeking something they now desire.

To effectively back up ad and PR efforts, your sales need to be somehow related to the ad or story. For example, you don't want to sell tanning bed packages as part of a cancer research fundraiser, but you may want to sell spray tanning or self-tanning packages and products.

As we discussed in the previous chapter, sales often take a traditional form – buy one, get one; buy the product suite and get X free – but we want you to think outside the box and find ways to bring in new clients and build a loyal base of clients.

One mistake that many retailers make with sales and specials is not capturing that customer and converting them into a loyal client who will stay with you for a long period of time. There are a number of ways to bring a customer back and turn them into a loyal, return client, and one way is to offer sales and specials that include a package of services that compels the client to return over time.

Think strategically about your sales and specials and be sure they are seasonally appropriate, product or service focused, bring clients back into the salon, competitively priced and profitable.

- Offer a free bottle of expensive nail polish with the purchase of a four-manicure package. It gets a product in (and on) their hands and it gets them in the door four times, giving you four opportunities to convince them your salon is the place to be.

- Offer a free blow out for your best clients on slower days. What a great way to get clients back in your styling chair. Make sure to use plenty of hair spray and upsell them on the spray or other product you use in their hair. Remember, the blow out is free, the product is not.

- Sell cut and color combinations at a discount for first time clients and include a "between appointments shape up" that removes the dead ends and keeps hair looking and feeling healthy and beautiful. The shape up trim would only take a few minutes and it shows them you care how they look and feel. Even better, it only takes a few minutes time for each stylist and, since not everyone will participate but everyone will remember it, there's not much time lost in this freebie.

Things to Think About

1. Do you have the skills and knowledge to create an effective ad for your salon?

2. Have you identified the right people with the right skills (photographer, graphic designer, writer) to help you create an effective ad if you need them?

3. What is your marketing budget?

4. Do you have the skills and knowledge to write and distribute an effective press release?

5. Have you identified someone who can help you with a press release if necessary?

6. Have you considered the following topics for press releases:
   - New Business Openings
   - New Hires
   - New Services
   - Expansion of Store
   - New Location
   - New Equipment
   - Charity/Outreach Efforts
   - Haircare and Beauty Tips

7. Have you identified a local magazine, section of the newspaper or blog to work with on makeovers or photo shoots? Have you reached out to them?

8. Have you identified any local designers or models in need of a stylist for an upcoming runway show?

9. Have you developed packages designed to get clients to return?

10. Are your sales and specials appropriate for the season and occasion?

CHAPTER 26

The Sales Representative Relationship

"It's not what you tell them…it's what they hear."

—Red Auerbach

In Chapter 23 we covered communicating with clients, here we want to talk about maintaining retail relationships, specifically, how to communicate with your product vendors, providers, distributors and manufacturers.

By developing an appropriate bond with your sales representatives, you'll benefit from far more than just promptly returned calls or hassle-free service; you'll also tap into their insider's network of sales tips and tactics.

Remember, they've been dealing with a number of salons and have seen more plans succeed and fail than you can imagine and you can benefit from their experience. If you have the right relationship, that is.

Why You Need a Strong Vendor Relationship

Your primary relationship as a retail salon is with your clients. They're bringing in the money, the bodies, the recommendations and the sales, so you should do whatever you can (within reason) to keep that relationship alive and well. The second most important business relationship you have may well be with your sales representatives.

A strong relationship with your sales representatives has many potential benefits for your salon and can end up being an asset to your business. Have you thought about product returns, new product lines, payment terms, delivery? So, have they.

Building Your Vendor Relationship

Building your sales representatives relationship is not unlike building any friendship – find the common ground and take it from there. You and your sales representatives have built in common ground – the product – the rest can grow from there.

Find out about their interests, their personal life, and their past. In that information, you'll find common ground and places to bond.

It's important to remember to listen more than you talk; that gives you the information

How a strong relationship with your sales rep can help

- **Product Returns** – Many times, suppliers will have restocking fees for returned merchandise. If you and your sales representative are on good terms (and you've been diligent about paying in full, on time, every time), they may be able to waive restocking fees, shipping or other charges/ penalties associated with returning unused or unsold products.

- **New Product Lines** – Imagine being the first salon on the block to have a product or tool. With a good working relationship, you can be the first person your vendor things of when approaching clients about exclusive or semi-exclusive products. At the very least, they may give you extra samples or test products to use and demonstrate at no cost.

- **Payment Terms** – As long as you've been maintaining your account and it's in good standing, your sales representative may be able to work with you on payment terms for products your salon needs. They may be able to extend a line of credit to you rather than ask for payment up front, which would allow you to put product on the shelves and in the hands of clients, which puts money in the bank which lets you pay the vendor in full.

- **Product Delivery** – Having trouble expediting an order? A quick call to your sales representative can help put the product on your shelves within 24 hours. Your vendor can also help with shipping costs and put in a rush order when your supply hits critical low points.

- **Business Partner** – Most distributor/manufacturers like L'Oreal have business associates they can recommend for credit card processing, financing, software consulting and more. Often, these partner services can be paid for based on your purchase history with the company.

- **Education** – Educating your team is important and your distributors and sales representatives often offer training on new and existing retail products and services that highlight their brand.

- **Displays** – Many companies have their own branded displays and racks for retail products. With a good sales representative relationship, you can get these for a discounted rate depending on your sales levels and relationship.

you may need later to make an informed decision on how to proceed with your vendor. By this, we mean that you should take your cues from the vendor. If they're funny and joking, be funny and joking back; if they're all business, keep the small talk small and get to it; if they're open to talking about their family, life or history, be open to sharing yours.

It comes down to this piece of advice: treat others how you would like to be treated.

And this one: smile.

Remember, you don't have to be best friends with your sales representative, but you should be friendly, on a professional level, and have a good rapport with them.

Some things to keep in mind when communicating with sales reps

- Sales representatives are people too. Treat them with respect and kindness and they'll treat you the same.

- Sales representatives are busy. Like you, they have multiple clients and aren't always able to drop what they're doing and switch tasks. How do you feel when demanding clients come in the salon? Don't make your vendors feel the same way you do.

- A little patience, understanding and empathy go a long way. Give sales representatives time to answer emails and return phone calls.

- Be honest with sales representatives about product orders, pricing and payment options because they may have creative options at their disposal. If you're having trouble meeting a minimum, they may have another client in the same situation and you may be able to split an order to reach minimums.

- Be open to conversation. No, you don't need to spend 30 minutes chatting it up with a sales representative, but a little personal talk can go a long way to solidify a relationship.

- Remember that sales representatives don't own delivery companies, so give them a break if your order doesn't make it the next day. Most times it isn't their fault.

Did You Know Your Distributor/Manufacturer Sales Person Can:

- Assist in scheduling advanced training for your team
- Arrange for a top stylist to visit your salon
- Order new promotional material for your retail area
- Assist with business decisions and relationship building that can strengthen your business

Trade Secrets - Retail Do's and Don'ts

We may call them "no no's" but they're more guidelines than rules. These tips can help increase sales and improve the client experience. And, as they become habit, your employees will learn a lot of what it takes to be a professional.

- Greet everyone who comes through the door. A warm hello makes them feel at home and gives them a taste of the vibe in your salon.

- Keep negativity to yourself. Avoid saying things are slow or dead, the day was draining, et cetera.

- Be positive. When clients ask about your day, tell them a positive experience rather than a negative one.

- Leave your troubles at home. No client wants to hear about your troubles. If they're friends, talk to them after work.

- When customers inquire about a product or service, "No" is not an acceptable answer unless you follow it with "but we have/I can do…"

- "I don't know" is not an acceptable answer either unless you follow it with "but I'll find out for you."

- Don't be condescending. It seems obvious (and we know you and your employees would never do it on purpose), but saying things like "No problem" rather than "You're welcome" makes you come across as cold and uncaring.

- Don't ask yes or no questions. Always ask questions that encourage clients to talk. Rather than asking, "Is there anything else you'd like to pick up today?" ask, "What kinds of products are you using now?" and then suggest complimentary or improved products.

- Always suggest an item that complements the client's purchase or treatment. This is an easy sales tactic that works.

- A positive personal appearance is a must. Dress nicely, but not outrageously, and always put yourself together before reporting to work. And, above all else, smell good – don't walk in smelling like a cigarette, alcohol or something else unpleasant.

- Don't show clients your frustration. It's hard to do and sometimes things aren't going the way you want them to. Take a breath, collect yourself, focus on something positive and then complete the task at hand.

- Don't hide behind the reception desk or salon chair. Guide clients to the products you recommend and sell with a personal touch.

- Unless absolutely necessary, don't restock products with clients in the store. Grab a couple of things you need to restock, stash them behind the counter and stock them as soon as clients are out of the line of sight.
- Remember to keep your service, smile and welcoming attitude even after the client has paid. Thank them for their patronage and wish them a good day.

Ready, Set, Go! Trade Secrets

Close More Sales With These Tips

- Never sell a product, sell a solution. Tell your clients: "In order to get this look, you need this product." Then introduce the product, tell how and why it works and demonstrate how to use it.

- When selling to men, don't overwhelm them with details, instead, zero in on their needs and the benefits of the product you recommend. Present it to them as a solution (as above) rather than a product.

- Male clients often don't know what sort of style they're looking for or how to achieve it with a product at home. By keeping out a style book (often available from product vendors), you can recommend a style and appropriate product to your male clients.

- Sell seasonally. In the summer, push products like detoxifying shampoos and nourishing conditioners. Tell clients, "In the summer, we put our hair through a lot of abuse. Between the chlorine in the pool and the salt in the ocean and the damage of the sun, it's important to strip the impurities and strengthen the hair. It makes hair more healthy and makes your color last longer."

- Allow clients to interact with the products – let them smell it, touch it, even apply it (in some cases).

- Walk to the reception desk with your client. Along the way stop and pick up a product you recommend they use. Walk to the desk with them and leave it there on the counter for them.

- Have fun. Use a prescription pad to communicate the best products to your clients. Write them the prescription, go to the retail zone with them and introduce the products and solutions to the clients.

- Ask your clients what their ideal product would do for them, then recommend a product (or suite of products) that provide the solutions they're seeking.

- Follow up after the sale and see if your clients need a little refresher (or some initial "training") in applying their product.

- Go for the soft sale. Rather than selling a product, recommend one. This softer approach often yields good results with hesitant or reluctant clients.

Social Media and Web Tools A Successful Salon Retail Business Must Use

Facebook

- You can use it for personal or business purposes
- You can import your contact list to search for current Facebook friends
- Personal page
- Up to 5,000 friends
- Privacy controls
- Share photos and video
- Can group your friends into lists
- Minimal customization; however, custom tabs and applications can allow for a more personalized look of your page to reflect your personal brand

Business Page on Facebook

- No limit on number of fans
- Fans don't have to join to see information
- Can control fan interaction (wall posts, etc.)
- Share photos and video
- Bulk messages to fans goes to "updates" and not "inbox messages"
- Statistics on demographics of fans and interactions
- Can personalize applications (e-commerce, custom tabs, etc.)
- Administrators are private, meaning you can hire outside help to keep your page up and running or share the administration with a couple of people

YouTube

- Video sharing
- Can make videos public, unlisted, or private
- Can make videos available to specific users
- Provides embedded HTML codes for adding videos onto any website
- You can create an automatic feed of newly uploaded videos into your website
- You can customize your YouTube channel page to your salon's brand

LinkedIn

- Used primarily for business purposes
- More professional users
- Resembles an online resume

- You can import your contacts and search for current LinkedIn users
- You can integrate your Twitter updates to post automatically to your LinkedIn update
- You can search by individual's name, company, title, location etc.
- "Answers" application allows you to position yourself as an expert
- "Polls" application allows you to create polls and share them on and off of LinkedIn
- You can join groups to ask and answer questions

Twitter

- Referred to as a "micro-blogging" website
- Users are limited to 140 characters in their updates
- Personalization of Twitter page for branding
- Can group the people you follow into lists
- Can "direct message" (private message) individuals
- Mostly used to quickly update followers or send links to relevant information or external sites
- By adding a # before a word, you make it searchable within Twitter (keywords)
- Can reply to someone publicly, for example: @sourcesalonspa
- Courtesy is to "retweet" information others post and to follow back those who follow you

Here are some other tools to consider:
- Tweetdeck: updates Facebook and Twitter simultaneously
- Hootsuite: allows you to schedule posts across multiple social media channels

Here are our best recommended practices for these social networks:
- Combine your social media efforts with your website
- Repurpose your blog into your social media
- Drive traffic to your website via social media and capture user details
- Include social media icons (links) on your website to your social media pages

Blogs

- Blogs are like an online diary, only in this case don't talk about recent breakups or other personal information, talk about your industry and build your credibility
- They are used to share information in a less formal way
- You can blog about inspiration, business, family, causes, or just about anything you wish
- You can tie in your blog to your website

Web Presence & Social Marketing

- They continue to grow in popularity
- Great for SEO (Search Engine Optimization)
- Aside from our home page, we notice that our blog is the second most-visited page on our website

Business Listings

List your business on the following sites

- Yelp
- Foursquare
- Yellowpages
- Google+
- Yahoo Local
- Manta

Other Tools

- MailChimp – an easy, template based tool for an email newsletter. Free for newsletters up to 2,000 subscribers
- Constant Contact – like MailChimp, but with a monthly fee
- Microsoft Outlook – for those of you using Microsoft's office tools, Outlook has a newsletter template and mail list function that works well once you establish your design and format

PART VI

TECHNOLOGY IN THE SALON

CHAPTER 27

The Tech Savvy Salon

"Computers and software are now the backbone of small business, but selling and servicing the customer enables us to buy the computers and software we need. Remember, the customer is king."

—Jeff Grissler

We spoke with two experts in salon software systems to hear about what specialized software can provide for your salon. John Harms of Harms Software, offers Millennium, a powerful software package that can bring a lot what you want to your salon. Anthony Spotorno, owner of EnnoView, offers an equally powerful set of software that can help you take your salon to new heights. Read on to see what these two had to say about software solutions for your salon and see how well it integrates with retailing and customer retention.

Here's what John Harms of Harms Software has to say about Millennium.

Salon Software and Retailing

Tracking inventory used to be "guess work" and ordering retail products was more of a gut feeling than a science. Salon software takes a lot of that headache away and gives you more accurate ordering and knowledge you simply wouldn't have without a computer system. The computer will know exactly what you need to order in seconds based on the model quantities and order points you establish for each of your products. Because the software knows how many of each product you have you will get instant access to your inventory value with a monthly history. This is very valuable so you can visually see if you're ordering is getting ahead of the buying trend causing you to accumulate too much inventory. Why leave that cash sitting on the shelf or in boxes? Salon software gives you an easy mechanism for counting inventory and tracking losses and theft as well. If you have more than one location look for a system that supports centralized inventory management including offsite purchase orders, warehousing, and the ability to manage inventory from multiple locations in a single application.

Selling retail with a salon software program has its advantages. Simply scan a product barcode and the product comes up instantly with the right price or sales price. Using inventory methodologies like FIFO (first in first out) the system will know exactly what you paid for the item being rung up and give you more accurate profit numbers. Why? Because you may have 24 bottles of shampoo in stock of which 12 were purchased 2 months ago at $5.99 each and then 12 more were purchased last month at $4.99 as a special from the distributor. Using First In First Out, the computer system will figure out that the bottle you just sold was most likely from the $5.99 order rather than the latest order of $4.99 each. Another concept is called Average Cost. The system can give you, on average, what the cost of your items are when you are determining profit. All of these great inventory features are part of a good computer system and would require a lot of people-power to do manually; if at all. This is a great feature giving valuable time back to the owner or manager for selling or other time-sensitive tasks.

Software like Millennium will show you exactly what the client usually buys and when they will need that product again. You can identify buying habits, run a promotion for 'anyone who bought xyz shampoo in the last 6 months', etc. Conversely, you could run a Slow Moving Product report that will identify items you might want to put on sale because they aren't selling. Another feature in Millennium, specifically, is a Product Retention report. This report will show you how often people buy and then rebuy a product or products.

Product history is important and a salon software system will track all your retail and cost price changes. You can see, by month, how much of a product you sold and watch for seasonality too. Commissions for employees are automatically calculated and you can even have incentives on certain products that allow a commission override and a reason to push certain products based on your needs or a distributor or manufacturer promotion.

THAT'S WHAT THEY SAY

When it comes to inventory control, Australian salon owner Steve Corthine of Stevie English Hair, learned a lesson and implemented the proper software to help him control product supply levels and costs.

"One of my biggest mistakes when I first opened my salon was lack of inventory control…A visit from my friend and fellow salon owner showed me the light. I had thousands of dollars tied up in unused inventory and our cash flow was suffering. He encouraged me to set proper inventory levels, process all stock through the computer, monitor waste and take inventory regularly."

Setting sales goals for retail but also tracking units sold per guest is a great idea. Salon software can show you, on average, how many units a client buys. An example would be .5 units per guest (meaning about ½ the clients are buying retail). Another metric is revenue per guest in retail. So you can see which employees are doing their cross sell of shampoo AND conditioner or who is selling the more expensive items or styling tools.

Salon software should also allow you to create client loyalty systems around retail. Give 1,000 points for buying certain products or points for purchasing at least $50 in product. Clients can then redeem points for an item when they obtain enough points. This keeps them interested in retail and coming back for more.

Computer software is essential to accuracy in inventory management, fast point of sale lookup, and your ability to market and report on retail sales. Some software companies preload product lines for you to help make the setup process faster. Do your homework and find out which software is best for you based on features, price, their ability to support you when you need help, how long they've been in the beauty industry, and what kind of ongoing education they provide.

Here's some information from Anthony Spotorno of EnnoView, a salon software provider.

Software solutions for effective retail management

We all know how important it is to sell retail and the true success of the salon lies with the retail sales. Now it is time to learn that Salon Software is the key to inventory control as well as tracking and using your database to drive your retail promotions to the right clientele.

You hear all the time. Just sell more retail, like it is that easy! How will software help you sell more retail you ask? That truly is easy to answer in four simple words: control, track, promote and plan. With salon software, all of this is possible. Good software will not only allow you to enter your on hand inventory but will allow you to order based on preset minimums and maximums as well as order based on what sold over a period of time.

Selling retail with the right software is simple. All manufacturers use a universal barcode system and by using a barcode scanner integrated with your software selling and tracking your retails sales becomes a breeze. The right software will store the customers' product history and allow you to watch trends of your sales on a regular basis with proper reporting features.

Running retail promotions with the right software system is key to any successful business. Having the history of your clients, you can send marketing email blasts to customers based on past purchases and favorite items. Using only a paper tracking system, promotions are impossible.

Inventory planning is an extremely important piece of the retail

Building and making clients and retail sales are some of the salon's biggest challenges. The good news is that by having great sales, inventory tracking, booking and client relationship management software and some tech-savvy stylists will make this process so much easier.

puzzle. With the reporting of sales trends and inventory purchase orders and a receiving system it is safe to say you will be able to have your finger on the pulse of your inventory levels at all times. Having an inventory valuation report gives you on hand counts and the value of all of your retail on hand which is a must have.

In closing, I am sure you will agree that having the right software solution for your business is an investment that will prove to be one that will continue to have positive returns over and over again.

Accounting

The one thing we didn't really touch on yet in this chapter is accounting.

Get with your accountant or tax preparer ahead of time and see what software they use – it will be Quickbooks, Quicken or Peachtree, most likely – and get a copy for yourself. All of these pieces of accounting software allow you to print invoices, checks, statements and financial reports, and stay on top of your finances.

Be sure you ask your salon software provider:
- Is there an application fee?
- Is there a programming or setup fee?
- What are the "other" fees associated with my merchant account?
- Are the quoted rates guaranteed? If so, for how long?
- Is there a contract? If so, for how long?
- Are there any termination fees or early cancellation fees?
- If there is a problem, who do I talk to?
- How long do processed payments take to reach my bank account?
- Are there any reserve requirements or hold backs? Can I get that in writing?
- What are the hours of operation for customer service?

CHAPTER 28

Salon Computer Hardware Needs

For your salon to really take advantage of the software and cloud-based applications (the "cloud" is the internet, so they're remote-access applications), you're going to need some hardware to run it. Let's look at some of the tools you might need to purchase and some of the questions you might have about technology.

Computers

- **Do I need a "real" server?**

  No. If you are just looking to have a small network without online booking or an online store, you can use a fileserver or robust workstation to act as your server.

  Larger network servers are recommended for:

  Five or more computers

  Several open connections for online booking

  Multiple and different types of software running at the same time

- **How many workstations should I get?**

  The answer depends upon the amount of staff and space you have. In an average-sized salon, there would be two computers at the front desk for reservations and check out and another computer in the back for a look-up station and to import service notes for the staff.

- **Do I need a computer in the backroom?**

  It is highly recommended to eliminate clutter and personnel swarming at the front desk by having a "look-up station" in the back of the salon. Your front desk is a client's first impression. It's best to eliminate as much chaos at the front desk as possible. When employees have a source of checking on appointments and monitoring their metrics, it promotes a more relaxed atmosphere and more informed service providers.

Network

- **Wired or wireless?**

  Wired networks are ideal in most scenarios. The data transfer rate is higher and it requires less maintenance than a wireless network. However, wireless networks can be used with tools like Microsoft® Terminal Services and ThinSoft® WinConnect®, allowing you to use portable tablet PCs or eliminate the clutter of wired stations.

- **Should I get an Internet connection?**

  The Internet is essential to taking advantage of email and social media marketing, remote backups, and for doing automated updates. It is also an essential element to allow remote support by your software company.

Peripheral Equipment

- **Cash Drawers:** You can choose between USB and serial cash drawers. It is suggested that you purchase USB drawers, as most computers don't come with serial ports anymore. Cash drawers add a layer of security to your front desk because they are locked unless the computer opens the drawer. Each time that occurs, the software you choose should track it in an activity log for your review.

- **Receipt Printers:** Most receipt printers work well with salon software. You may want to purchase a receipt printer that has a mechanism to automatically open your cash drawer, which will allow you to purchase a non-intelligent drawer and save money.

- **Other equipment:** You might consider a credit card swipe that mounts on the side of your monitor; pole displays to show what the client is purchasing (this is a requirement in certain states or counties); paging systems that alert staff when a client checks in; and more. You might be surprised at all the options you have once you computerize.

Controlling costs and staying within your budget can be challenging when you start purchasing the computers and peripherals you need. Don't worry, we have some suggestions that can help your bottom line and keep your budget in tact.

Computers

Saving money buying computers is as easy as buying a full-priced model. Apple and Dell both offer outlets and refurbished units via their online stores. In these online stores, you can get upwards of 25% off the regular price. Both Apple and Dell sell their full suite of products – laptops, ultrabooks, desktops – online, according to availability.

Apple: http://store.apple.com/us/browse/home/specialdeals/mac

Dell: http://www.dell.com/outlet/

Network

If you're going to be using a network, it's advisable to have an IT consultant help you set it up. But if all you need is a wireless router and some external storage to use as backup, there are plenty of places that will lead you to deals, reviews and advice on purchasing this equipment.

Head to gizmodo.com, lifehacker.com or cnet.com for reviews and recommendations on networking solutions. All three of these sites are easy to navigate. Simply search on their site for whatever it is you need and you'll find some solid information.

Peripheral Equipment

For things like cash registers, cash drawers and receipt printers, find your local used business equipment seller and check their inventory of cash registers and drawers. Depending on what you need, they may have it on hand, if they don't, they'll keep an eye out for you and contact you when they find one.

For online shopping, americanrefurb.com sells a variety of refurbished office equipment including cash registers, copiers, fax machines, printers, shredders, time clocks, credit card terminals and more.

Music

There's no doubt about it, you're going to want music in your salon. Fortunately, with all of the iPods and iPhones and online music players, there are a lot of great options that will set you back very little.

For the most basic sound system you'll need a receiver (it controls the volume and where the music comes from), several speakers and a connection to your computer or mp3 player. Crutchfield.com is a great outlet to find refurbished pieces of stereo equipment like receivers and speakers. Their expert-written articles can help you understand some of the complexities you encounter when pulling together a large sound system like this.

Your salon must:

1. Be wireless
2. Sell retail at events
3. Allow stylists to sell retail
4. Allow stylists to book appointments
5. Have clearly defined goals

As for the music coming out of your speakers, look no further than your iPod or other mp3 player to bring in music from your own collection. To take it a step further, look online at services like Pandora, rdio and spotify, they have a variety of free and paid subscriptions to their vast music libraries.

CHAPTER 29

The Ins and Outs of Credit Card Payment Processing

"Remember that credit is money."

—Benjamin Franklin

For this chapter, we decided to lean on the expertise of Guy Wadas, National Sales Director for Integrity Payment Systems. His company provides credit card payment processing and his knowledge of the industry is vast.

Understanding credit card processing and knowing how to leverage its advantages can have a dramatic, profitable impact for salon owners. Choosing the wrong credit card processor or not understanding the best way to structure your processor agreement can be a constant monthly drain on your business.

Most businesses—no matter how large or small—make very small profits on a percentage basis. Knowing how to increase your profits—even by a percentage point or two—can provide the difference between "getting by" and enjoying a business which provides you with the lifestyle you want.

Following is an overview of the reasons to accept credit cards, the costs and benefits of credit card processing, how to select the right processor, and what questions to ask before signing any agreement. At the end of the chapter, we will also provide a list of unique programs offered to salon owners by one credit card processing company, including a free assessment of your current costs.

Why Accept Credit Cards?

For some barbershop owners, operating on a strictly cash basis seems like the least costly way to operate. No processing fees, no equipment to buy—and, it seems clean and simple. In fact, in the early 1990s, more than 80 percent of the money coming into hair, beauty, and grooming businesses was in the form of cash. Now, however, that number has flipped and more than 80 percent of the money comes in through credit or checking/debit cards. Why the switch? It's all about convenience for the client and the potential additional profits.

Everything has a cost. Identifying the cost of credit card processing on the balance sheet is easy to do. What is not easy is to identify the cost of NOT accepting credit cards in your business. Several studies have shown that clients are willing to spend more when paying with credit than when paying with cash. In fact, when J.C. Penney Company, Inc. started to accept credit cards in its stores several years ago, it found that the average transaction for credit clients was $50 compared to cash transactions of only $20. People are not carrying cash these days; instead, they want the convenience of paying with credit or debit cards.

Salon owners can capitalize on this by offering products to their clients as well as add-on services. When paying with credit, clients are much more likely to purchase a service package, gift certificates/cards, as well as retail. Walk-in clients are also likely to prefer to pay with credit by the same 80/20 ratio. Referring these clients to a nearby ATM machine sends the message that you are more concerned about your convenience than your clients. Many will not come back to an establishment that does not accept payment via credit/debit card. The cost of NOT accepting credit may be the loss of sales in additional products and services over months and years, and you could lose the 80 percent of clients who no longer prefer to pay with cash.

If it makes sense to accept credit and debit card payments in your barbershop, how do you make sure you do this in a way that is best for you, rather than your bank or a third-party processor?

Choosing the Right Processor

Your local bank may provide credit processing either directly or through a third-party processor. You can also contract directly with a processor like Integrity Payment Systems. Who you choose for this important process can make a huge difference in your bottom-line profits.

Most local banks outsource this service to a third party that has an agreement or arrangement with the bank. A few national banks process credit transactions themselves. Regardless, you need to ask several key questions in order to make sure you have the best program for your business.

If the processing is outsourced, it is likely the customer service will also be outsourced. That can create a very frustrating situation should you have a problem or question. Look for a full-service credit card processor that handles not only the sales, but also the back-end processing, customer service, and other functions. They will be the most secure when it comes to protecting your clients' sensitive credit card information. They will also be the most responsive should you ever have an issue.

Is the Lowest Rate Always Best?

Most processors will quote a rate for processing transactions and position a rate that is one of the lowest rates available. What they do not tell you about are the additional fees involved, including a substantial cancellation or early-termination fee designed to keep you locked into the contract even after you find a better provider. Low rates can be deceiving. Be sure you understand all the terms in the contract.

You want to get to a number called "total cost" or "effective rate." That number includes not only the low rate, but also all of the add-on charges, fees, and other costs. The effective rate is the number that matters, not the initial rate.

Card companies such as Visa, MasterCard, Discover, and American Express set different rates for different cards, industries, and customers. These rates are called interchange. They are numerous, and to further complicate the picture, these rates range anywhere from a zero percentage rate with a small per-item fee, to levels that include a percentage rate greater than three percent with large per-item fees. Unless you are working with a company that specializes in the hair, beauty, and grooming industry, it is unlikely you will be able to obtain the most favorable rates for your business. In fact, you will most likely be quoted the same rates and pricing structures as the car repair shop down the street. One size does not fit all, and one rate for all businesses is not going to fit either.

Integrity Payment Systems has been monitoring the flow of transactions for the hair, beauty, and grooming industry for many years. Your barbershop will not be lost in their system, as they have a dedicated in-house division that tracks and examines the interchange rates specifically for thousands of salon/barbershop businesses across the nation. Acquiring this data has enabled the exceptional ability to verify that barbershop owners are being charged correctly and at the best rate for their specific business.

Does the Processor Understand the Salon Business?

Another indicator of an appropriate credit card processor for your business is how well the company understands the salon business and the challenges you face. If the credit card processor is endorsed by respected industry partners such as Redken, Pureology, L'Oreal Professional, Matrix, Mizani and others, it is a good sign that they offer a mix of services and products that will be most appropriate for your business. Other endorsements to look for include the Summit Salon Business Center (the largest salon consulting firm), The Salon Professional Academy schools, State Beauty Supply, RDA ProMart distributor stores, and Salon Centric (the largest salon product distribution hub in America).

Beyond the endorsements of industry professionals, barbershop owners should be aware of additional programs and services tailored exclusively to the owner's business needs. For example, Integrity Payment Systems (which is endorsed by the above-mentioned salon industry companies and more) has created four unique services to help create a successful and profitable business. Salon owners control each of these services and direct each of the percentages, which include:

1. **Auto-Save**: a system which helps salon owners build an emergency fund automatically by separating a small percentage of each transaction into their savings account.

2. **Pay-Fast Bill Payment**: helps salon owners automatically stay current with bills by directing a percentage of each transaction to payment of key vendors.

3. **Pay-Fast Debt Elimination**: eliminates debt by systematically directing a portion of each transaction to pay creditors.

4. **B.O.B.**: helps salon owners accurately anticipate costs, revenue, and other budget items to plan for profitability.

Because salon owners are part of the Integrity team, the company was able to look at issues affecting owners and devise helpful solutions that leverage the credit card processing technology.

Better management of credit and debit processing can add new clients and increase the average ticket size. With the help of special tools, salon owners can save for the future, pay off debts, and budget for improved profitability.

CHAPTER 30

Selecting the Right Phone System for Your Salon: Holding On for the Life or Death of Your Business

"We all have something to say and sometimes it's an easy transmission, sometimes it's not. Keep it simple! Keep it to the point and share your love and passion to the people who hear your phone tree and voicemail message."

—Jeff Grissler

We *asked Kris Olsen, the owner of Solutions on Hold, a phone system architect and provider to lend us some insight into how to select the perfect phone system.*

In the competitive salon and spa industry, we find most new and existing clients inquire about appointments, specials, services, and products via the telephone. What happens if your salon's front desk personnel are busy simultaneously answering telephone calls AND helping clients who're standing in front of them? Most of the time the answer is that the telephone call is placed on hold.

Hold is not always a negative. It's often a sign of a busy, successful business in action. While you attempt to take care of your in-salon guests, it's inevitable that you'll place calls on hold at this time. Below is a prescription that takes care of those callers while they wait and helps you promote your services, products, and special offers.

While many businesses try to keep customers and prospects on the line with radios, possibly playing a competitor's commercials, silence, beeps, or elevator music, successful marketers know that a professional message on hold program pays off. In fact, customers prefer to hear messages on hold and will stay on the line for over three minutes if they're listening to a well-done, professional program.

Conversely, 90 percent of callers will hang up within 40 seconds with silence. Hang-ups are expensive and there's no need to send callers and your future revenue stream to your competitors. Take the correct path and provide your callers a professionally produced, telephone message on hold program about your salon or spa.

The cost for this service is minimal compared to other forms of advertising and the benefits are exponential. The best on hold providers include the equipment, installation, and updates for rates from $49 to $99 per month. Rates are typically based on the amount of times you plan to update the program each year. The elite production companies will even send you ideas via regular contact to insure fresh and productive on hold content.

So what are the benefits of having a professionally produced, telephone "on-hold" program? Your clients and prospects stay on hold longer. You can thank them for their business and tell them about products, services, social media updates, and promotions available at your salon. Also, professionally produced "on hold" programs help your business seem more professional and polished.

Typically, this service is easy to get started with. Most quality "on hold" advertising companies have "Get Started" forms on their websites that enable you to enter important information about your salon and spa that you'd like to have communicated "on hold." The "on hold" company takes this information and writes a draft of a script for you to proofread. You'll usually be able to select voices and music at the website as well. Once you've proofread the script, made your corrections, and selected your voices and music the "on hold" company produces your program.

Usually your program will be emailed to you for review to ensure words are pronounced correctly and that the voices and music match your tastes. At this point, the "on hold" company will ship you a digital playback system that connects to your telephones or telephone system. Connecting the device is simple. However, if you're afraid to try it reputable "on hold" companies in many cases will pay a licensed telephone system vendor to connect it for you. Billing for a service like this is done monthly, quarterly, or all at once and like most businesses "on hold" companies accept credit cards, do bank withdrawals, or take company checks.

Now you're ready to make the most of your telephone message on hold time, so don't leave your callers hanging. Treat guests with respect by thanking them for their business and simultaneously boost your sales by promoting your salon and spa's fantastic products and services!

Remember:

- Longer hold times, fewer hang-ups
- THANK YOUR CUSTOMERS FOR THEIR BUSINESS!
- Promote products and services
- Advertise promotions
- Promote your Facebook, Twitter, and other social media accounts
- Introduce new service providers or employees
- Present the professional image of a large corporation

Solutions on Hold can be found on the web at:

www.solutionsonhold.com

www.solutionsonhold.net

www.telephoneprompts.com

Credit Card Processing Tips

In the chapter on credit card payment processing, Guy Wadas, National Sales Director for Integrity Payment Systems, gave a lot of great information to help you select a credit card payment processing company. Guy's intent, and ours, is to give you the information you need to make a well-informed decision and to minimize your risk as much as possible. That's why we've included this list of credit card processing tips. Guy already covered some of this, but us this along with the credit card processing chapter to make the best possible choice when entering into a relationship with a processing company.

1. **Never ask a sales representative "What's your rate?"**

   The full price you'll pay, and the pricing model the provider gets their rates from, involves more than the actual rate. The true rate include interchange passthroughs and other costs. The most important question to ask is "What's your pricing model?"

2. **Interchange pass through pricing works best.**

   Interchange pass through (sometimes called interchange plus pricing) is the least expensive, easiest-to-understand credit card processing model. It separates the actual cost of processing (interchange fees – charges that go to pay the issuing bank – and assessment fees – charges that pay the actual credit card company) from the processor's markup. The result of the transparent, easily understood billing is that you pay a lower markup, can see where the money is going and it keeps your processor from increasing costs by manipulating charges.

3. **Which is better, daily discount or monthly discount?** *Monthly discount.*

   Monthly discount is the better option by far. This is when processors take their charges in one lump sum at the end of each month. It's less expensive, easier to reconcile and better for your salon's cash flow.

4. **Never pay a cancellation fee.**

   Many credit card processors don't charge fees for cancelling your subscription to their service. Since this is the case, never enter into a relationship where they're asking you to pay to cancel. Ask your sales representative to waive the fee or move on to the next processor.

5. **You can – and should – get competitive rates.**

   Years ago, unless a business did a massive volume of credit card sales they couldn't get competitive rates on interchange pass through fees. Not any more. Shop around for the best deal; lower fees mean more money in your bank account.

6. **Which is better, quality or quantity? Quality wins.**

Focus your attention only on processors that advertise interchange plus pricing without cancellation fees (see tip number 4). Eliminating garbage fees like this makes the companies compete for your business and lets you make a fair comparison of their fees and pricing.

7. **Quickbooks' credit card processing is expensive.**

Yes, QuickBooks is among the best pieces of accounting software out there, but the credit card processing provided by Intuit (their parent company) is often priced significantly higher than competitors. The advantage is this: processing by Intuit is fully integrated into QuickBooks, competitors have software that interfaces with QuickBooks, but not as seamlessly. Ask yourself if it's worth the extra expense to integrate your credit card processing with QuickBooks.

8. **Just say no to tiered pricing.**

Tiered pricing (or bundled pricing) – how Intuit prices their processing services – is difficult to understand in part because your rates are based on three tiers (or more) of acceptance – like qualified, mid-qualified and non-qualified transactions – that may bring higher fees based on the terms of the contract. It's a bad deal, go with interchange pass through.

9. **Avoid proprietary credit card machines.**

Some processors will try to sell you a credit card machine that only works with their services. Don't do it. If you buy one of these and switch to a new processor, you'll be on the hook for a new machine. Instead, get a machine that can be reprogrammed by processors.

10. **Let the processing companies come to you for business.**

Before you ask a processing company sales representative a single question, tell them what you're looking for; don't ask them for the best deal they can give (you'll never get it). Tell them exactly what they need to do to earn your business. If they can't do it, find someone who can.

11. **Who do I go with, big businesses or small shops?**

Smaller operations, called independent sales organizations (ISO), offer rates that compete well with the bigger companies, but with an added benefit – as smaller companies, they'll have to fight harder and provide better service and support in order to earn and keep your business.

12. **If someone offers you a free credit card machine, say no.**

There's no such thing as a free credit card machine, the provider will always make up the fee for the machine with a higher percentage or some other fee.

13. **Never lease a credit card machine.**

Buy your machine from the start, it will cost between $100 and $500, but leasing it, which carries a monthly charge, can cost upwards of $3,000 for the same machine.

14. If a rate looks too good to be true, it is too good to be true.

As with free credit card machines, rates that seem impossibly low often are. These super low rates are often introductory rates that will escalate dramatically as time goes on.

15. Low rates are only half the battle.

The first step is getting a low rate, the second is keeping it. Read your statement every month. Your processor has to give you notice of any rate increases in your statement. If you see an increase come through, contact them and see how you can avoid it.

16. Get lower rates by being secure.

Using Visa's Verified by Visa and MasterCard's Secure Code programs, your business can help the credit card companies and issuing banks fight fraud and you can qualify for lower interchange pass through fees.

17. You only need one processing account.

For card present and card-not-present purchases, only one type of merchant account is needed. The only time you need two accounts is if your provider is trying to pull one over on you.

18. The only rate that matters – the effective rate.

The effective rate is the only thing that can accurately compare one provider's rates to another's'. If you paid $200 in fees during a month where you processed $10,000, your effective rate is 2%.

19. Can you pass along processing fees to your customers? Yes, if you're careful.

It's an accepted practice now to pass some of the processing fees long to customers, but you have to be careful in how you do it. Most (if not all) credit cards don't allow a convenience fee on credit card purchases, but you can offer a cash or check payment discount. For example: simply increase your base price by 10%, then offer a 10% discount for cash or check payment.

20. You can require a minimum purchase on a credit card…

Remember, you can impose a $10 minimum (the lowest you can currently go) on all credit card purchases.

21. …but not on debit card purchases.

Debit cards are exempt from the minimum charge rule for credit cards.

22. Check your statement – fees should be refunded for returns.

When a customer returns something and you put the credit back on their card, the processing company and credit card company should refund your fees for the initial transaction. Stay on top of this, especially if you have many returns.

23. Avoid "Big Box" processors.

Warehouse clubs like Costco, Sam's Club and the like offer credit card processing and merchant services through their club. Simply put, these programs push you toward tiered pricing and tack on a lot of additional fees and stipulations. It's best to avoid big box stores (see tip 11).

24. Understand your statement.

Be sure you understand your credit card statement. It may seem difficult or confusing at first, but call customer service and have a representative help you understand what you're seeing. Understanding your statement is key to identifying fee increases and profitability. The bottom line is this: don't be afraid to ask questions.

25. Credit card fees are tax deductible.

Check with your accountant, but as of the writing of this edition, credit card fees were tax deductible.

26. Size matters – ticket size, that is.

When it comes to transaction fees, the size of your ticket matters. Much of the profit from small tickets can be eaten away by transaction fees. If you have a small average sale, negotiate for the lowest rate possible, then start pushing more products and services (and consider raising costs) to bump up those tickets – it means more profit.

27. Your local bank isn't always best.

Your local bank is going to offer merchant services and credit card processing, but shop around, just because you have a checking account there doesn't mean they have the best rates or customer service.

28. Know your contract.

Many contracts will automatically renew at the end of the initial term. Know your contract so you can get out or renegotiate if you're unhappy with your service.

29. American Express plays by its own rules.

You'll see a number of businesses that don't accept American Express cards. That's because American Express sets their own fees. Unlike Visa and MasterCard, who allow other companies (banks, et cetera) to license their cards and distribute them, American Express does it all in house. Because they do that, they govern their own rates and charge a much higher fee for accepting their card.

30. Be sure you know and understand the answer before you agree to anything.

The only dumb question is the one you didn't ask, so avoid some heartache, headache and worry over money by asking all of your questions and finding the answers you want before you agree to anything with a credit card processing company (or any other company, for that matter). Be sure you understand the answers to all your questions. Be sure you're making an informed, educated decision.

What is a Typical Plan for Computerizing a Salon?

Unfortunately, there is not a one-size-fits-all solution when it comes to setting up your salon to be fully automated. Many factors, like size, number of network connections, and number of workstations (connected computers), affect the planning. However, you will take some definite steps and need to meet key milestones to get your technology infrastructure in place.

Phase I: Research

- Utilize the Internet to search for salon software or salon management software. You'll find dozens of options available to you. Look for companies that have been around for more than a couple of years and have shown a dedication to the beauty industry. Many companies come and go and you don't want to invest in a fly-by-night company.

- Ask around at industry events. What are other people using? Do they like it? Do they feel they get input into the updates? Does the company have annual conferences and attend industry-specific educational events?

Phase II: Demo/Testing

- Download a trial version of the software or request a demo.

- Schedule a live demonstration with a salesperson and gauge their knowledge of the beauty industry.

- Ask for the support phone number and try it a few times before you buy. Does someone answer? Do they know what they are talking about? Do they know the industry? Are they friendly and helpful?

Phase III: Software Selection

- After determining the top three software companies that fit your needs, you'll have to evaluate them on price, length of time in business, number of support staff, features/benefits of the software, and overall feeling you get for the company.

- Once you make a selection, it still takes a few phone calls and decisions before you're ready to start installing the software and entering data.

Phase IV: Hardware Needs Assessment

- It's best if you choose a company that is also knowledgeable in hardware, computers, and the other devices you'll need to run a successful salon.

- Ask for a needs assessment based on the size of your salon, size of your front desk, number of employees, and budget.

Phase V: Hardware Purchase

- Some computers, when special ordered, take a couple of weeks to ship. When they arrive, the software company can usually install the software for you. So, expect up to four weeks for computer delivery. It can come faster if the computers are in stock, but that's not always the case, especially during the busy season.

- During this phase, you should contact local computer service technicians to begin forging a relationship for ongoing support, computer setup, etc.

Phase VI: Network Setup

- You need to decide if you want to run wires for a wired network, which results in faster access to your data. However, if you want to run a wireless system, you will have to purchase computers and an operating system that will work best with a wireless system.

Phase VII: Software Installation

- Your software may be preinstalled on the computers you purchased from your provider. However, if you purchased the computers on your own, you'll need to install the software.

- Even if the software you are using is Web-based, there is still configuration and installation of drivers for your equipment.

Phase VIII: Data Entry Training

- Before you start entering data, take the time to get proper training or read the manual on how to enter the data properly.

Phase IX: Data Entry or Data Conversion

- Start pulling old invoices, purchase orders, and service menus together so you can enter them into the software you've purchased.

- Divide the work up amongst your staff so that everyone learns. However, make sure they enter the data consistently. It's important to make sure the data goes in properly so that the reports you run make sense.

Phase X: Advanced Training & Practice

- Now that your data is entered, you want to get advanced training on the appointment book, register, inventory, management, and security.
- Practice! Some software comes with the ability to create an instance of your data so you can train your employees and practice using the system without affecting the actual data.

Phase XI: Testing for "Go Live"

- Prior to going "live" and opening your salon for business with the new system, go through some sample ring-ups, bookings, payrolls, etc. to verify the system is functioning and set up properly.

Phase XII: "Go Live!"

- Fire up the computers and start booking appointments and ringing up all of those sales! Remember, partner with a software company that focuses on making the front desk a power position that helps grow the business!

— PART VII —

YOUR SALON

CHAPTER 31

Surviving the First Year

"Business is a combination of war and sport."

—Andre Maurois

One of the hardest things you'll ever do in your life is open a salon (or any business for that matter) and survive the first year. There will be plenty of sleepless nights; agonizing over finances large and small; arguments with business partners, employees, spouses and partners; times you're ready to walk away and never look back; and situations you never thought you'd find yourself it.

But don't let that scare you. After all, you wanted to open your own salon for a reason. You wanted to be the boss. You wanted to call the shots. You wanted the risk and the reward. And, believe us, there's plenty of reward.

- The first time a client recommends your salon to someone and they become a return customer.
- The first time your bank account says $1,000 (or more!) after you've paid the bills, met payroll and fulfilled your other financial responsibilities.
- The first time you look at your booking calendar and you don't see an empty space for two weeks or more.
- The first time someone tells you, "Great place you have here."
- The first time you hire and employee and say, "They remind me of me at that age; they've got what it takes to make it in this industry."

All of these things make the struggle worthwhile.

Remember that the struggle is part of the journey. Very rarely does a business open and become an overnight, and lasting, sensation. Many small businesses never become that overnight sensation, but they're around for 20, 30, even 40 years, and they bring the owners the financial stability and satisfaction of owning their own business.

Have you ever heard these two sayings:

If you break even in the first year, you're doing well.

If you survived the first year, you're on your way to becoming a successful business owner

They're both true. We're here as proof of it. It's not easy being authors and working in the salon finance industry and our beginnings were, like nearly everyone else's, humble, struggle-filled years where we inched and clawed our way toward lasting success. Now here we are, giving advice on starting your own successful salon in the latest installment in our successful book series.

In this chapter, we want to give you an idea of what to expect and how to adjust to the shifting sands of the business world during your first year. It's going to be a dizzying, heart-pounding time, but you've got what it takes. You can build a successful retail salon.

Stay on Budget

Where will your business be if you run over budget by just $500 a month? At the end of the year, you'll be $6,000 in debt, that's where. Trying to stay within a budget can be hard sometimes. You have responsibilities to meet: payroll, product orders, rent or mortgage payments, utilities (which can be quite high for salons), linens, payroll, business insurance, licenses (both professional and business), plus your pay. It's easy to go overbudget. It's easy to get overwhelmed. But, remember, it can be just as easy to meet your budget or even come in below budget and still deliver a high-quality salon experience.

During that first year of business, many entrepreneurs will spend all of (or even more than) their allotted budget, trying to force success on their business. You can't force it; success doesn't happen overnight (otherwise, we'd all just throw $50,000 at the problem and own successful businesses). Stick with a plan and adjust it as your finances change. Some months you may find yourself letting the belt out a notch, other months you'll tighten up, but with the right planning and execution, you can expect steady growth for your retail salon.

Here are some tips to help keep you and your salon on budget:

- Try to avoid unnecessary purchases. Every time you go to buy something – a piece of equipment, décor for the salon, tools, lunch – ask yourself if you really need it.
- Bring your lunch. You're an employee of the salon and you'll need to get paid. If you spend $10 a day on lunch and coffee/snacks (not an unreasonable amount), you'll spend $50 a week to eat. That comes out to $200 a month and $2,400 a year. If you bring in your lunch you'll eat healthier and stretch your (and your salon's) dollar further.

> *Tips*
>
> Developing a personal or household budget during this time is a good idea. It can help you control spending and provide more insight into what you need to earn to maintain your lifestyle.

- Stick with what you need. When ordering inventory, don't go out a buy a year's worth of product up front, even if you're offered a price break. What happens if it doesn't sell? You're stuck with product no one wants and no money in the cash drawer.

- Keep good records and review them weekly. Accurate financial records will allow you to easily trace every dollar spent by the salon. When you see wasteful spending, make a strong effort to curb it.

- Make a list, check it twice. Create a list of known monthly expenses (these are utilities (they may vary, but you can estimate an amount as long as you estimate high), rent/mortgage, payroll, money set aside for taxes and future purchases) then create a list of variable expenses (supplies, miscellaneous purchases). Estimate the costs if you need to. When you add everything up, you'll have a rough idea of your budget. As time goes on, and with good record keeping, you can adjust your numbers for a more accurate prediction and a develop a budget that's easier to keep.

- Review your budget (income and expenses) with someone every month. It doesn't matter if it is your bookkeeper, your business coach, your best friend, your spouse or partner, or your business partner. By reviewing your numbers with a third party you're building accountability into your accounting, and being held to your word to cut expenses or increase revenue will go a long way toward making it come true.

Keeping a budget does more than just keep your finances in order and keep you from falling into debt, it serves as a record of your salon's growth. In two years' time, if you apply for a Small Business Administration loan and can show them your well-kept financial records, you have a better chance of receiving the loan. The same applies to credit extensions with vendors. The same applies for grants, entrepreneur awards, business recognition programs and so much more.

Product Supply Credit

Unless you have the cash upfront to lay out for your product purchases, you're going to need a line of credit extended to you by your vendors and suppliers. This allows you to buy retail products and pay back their cost in monthly payments (although some vendors/suppliers work differently, check with each one to see how they work with financing and credit). Doing this will allow you to budget more accurately for your product expenses.

Remember: buy only what you need and do not go overboard with purchases. As your sales increase, your cash flow will increase and you can afford to buy more products.

You will also want to build a strong relationship with your product vendors and distributors and try to get the exclusive right to carry certain products or product lines. Competition is healthy, but not if someone next door is carrying the exact same thing.

Don't Be Afraid to Change

Ask anyone who has had a failed startup business and they'll tell you that their inability to acknowledge what was going wrong and make the necessary changes was a big contributor to killing their dream of business ownership. Don't be that guy.

With an accurate budget and a regular meeting to review numbers (with a partner or trusted individual), you'll have a realistic picture of where your business is. Once you have this information at your disposal, you can analyze it and see where you need to make adjustments. If there are things in your salon that seemed like a good idea but aren't bringing in the revenue you expected, make a focused effort to change that or get rid of them. Don't throw your hard-earned money at something that doesn't work.

If you see something in your business that needs tweaked, changed, overhauled, dumped or replaced, don't be afraid to do it. And sooner is always better than later when it comes to making decisions that affect your bottom line.

Learning During the First Year and Beyond

The first year is a learning curve. During this time you'll come to know a lot more about your market, neighborhood, business acumen, clients, products and yourself.

If you see someone doing something in their business that you find interesting or that you think would work well in yours, ask about it (the worst thing they can tell you is "no").

As we pointed out just a moment ago, keep yourself open to change. Listen to the suggestions of your vendors, employees and clients. They'll let you know what services they love and what ones they want; what products they want more, and less, of; what you're doing well and where you can improve. Listen to them and learn what you can do better.

Keep up with the latest trends in the industry and learn about salon management as well as small business success strategies. Attend trade shows, Small Business Association seminars, events put on by the local Chamber of Commerce or economic development council; network with other business owners at local business groups; be friendly with other salon owners.

Focus on Your Core Business

To succeed, you need to know what you're working towards. Ask yourself, "What is my salon's core business? What are my unique value propositions (what do I offer that clients can't find elsewhere)? What do I want my salon to be known for?" Questions like these will help you focus on your salon's mission and execution as you work toward becoming the salon of choice in your area.

One reason you have to focus goes back to the old saying: He's a jack of all trades and a master of none. This means you can do a little bit of everything, but you're mediocre (at best) at everything. Does this mean you need to be hyper focused and only offer coloring, no cuts or styling? Of course not, it just means you have to be the best at coloring and still offer exceptional cuts and styles. This means you'll need to hire talented people, possibly segmenting your salon into stylists and colorists.

When you've identified your core business (again, keep asking yourself, "What do I want my salon to be known for?"), you'll be able to look at the essential elements your business needs to succeed and help you achieve your goals. If your salon focuses on color, then some key elements of your business needs could be:

- A well-equipped coloring station (or stations)
- Top talent in your colorists
- Exceptional stylists (who also know about color, but whose passion is in the cut and style)
- Marketing materials (ads, flyers, social media, et cetera) that focus on your coloring talent, products and treatments
- Room for storage, equipment and clients
- Ongoing training for your employees
- Top of the line products to support your in-salon color line (these could be touch up kits, special shampoos and conditioners, et cetera)
- A great relationship with your color product vendor (or vendors)

One big mistake first-year business owners make is promising too much, then having trouble on the delivery. If you say you're doing the best coloring jobs in town, you better be able to back it up because someone will challenge your claim.

Tied to this is the idea of growth. We all look at our businesses and we see what we want them to be 2 years, 5 years, 10 years out and we get discouraged when we aren't there in our third month of operation. Don't let that get to you. When you set clear goals, focus on the core of your business and work your way toward profitability you have something to be proud of. Your dream salon may have 10 chairs, a dedicated coloring team, estheticians offering their services, make up consulting and teams to do hair and makeup for weddings, but the reality is that you have two chairs and a part-time massage therapist. That's fine. Work toward your goals. As you can afford it, you can lease the space next door, knock down the wall and put in two more chairs and a manicure/pedicure station. Then work toward the next goal.

Growth in business appears very slow to those on the inside (that would be you). If you find yourself discouraged about your growth or about how far you've come, throw yourself a five-minute pity party, then get a trusted advisor on the phone and tell them how you feel. Ask them to tell you how you're doing. You'll be surprised at how far you've come and at how many struggles you've worked through. Believe us, some of those struggles will seem impossible when you encounter them that first year, but when you look back later, you'll wonder what you even worried about.

CHAPTER 32

Startup Mistakes

"The important thing is not being afraid to make a mistake. Remember, the greatest failure is not to try."

—Debbie Fields

It's easy to make a mistake. The hard part is learning your lesson, cleaning up the mess and going on with things (oh, and not making it again, of course). Here are some common mistakes entrepreneurs like you make when starting their businesses.

1. **Going it Alone.** You may be a single-chair salon, but you still need a supporting cast. Don't isolate yourself in the business. Friends and colleagues who are in the same business, another business or no business at all are there to help. Just ask.

2. **Failing to Plan is Planning to Fail.** Identify your goals at different points (where is your salon in 6 months, 1 year, 2 years, 5 years) and develop a plan to reach them. Without a plan, it's easy to get off track and move away from your salon's core business.

3. **Marketing Mistakes.** From doing no marketing and wondering why no clients are coming in to doing too much marketing and getting more clients than your salon could ever handle, marketing mistakes come in many forms. When it comes to marketing, plan. Know your ideal client – where they shop, what they wear, what perfume/cologne they like, where they eat, what they read and watch, how much money they make, what their profession is/was – and plan to reach them. A common mistake is developing an ad (or a series of ads) and placing them in the wrong places.

4. **You're a Quitter.** When you encountered one hardship, you quit. Don't be a quitter. Find a way around the problem (even if that problem means dissolving the business and starting from scratch), you'll feel better about yourself when you look back at how you succeeded in the face of hardship.

5. **No Unique Selling Point.** Something has to differentiate you from your competition; this is your unique selling point. What are you doing that different from and better than the competition? Are you answering a unique need in the community, offering an innovative solution to a problem or are you just like every other salon? Identify the things that set you apart from the competition, those are your unique selling points.

6. **Being a Control Freak.** Your salon is your baby and it's natural to want to manage every aspect of the business down to the tiniest thing. This is called micromanaging and it's no good for anyone involved. If you exercise too much control, the business hinges entirely on you. If that's the case, what happens when you're sick and out from work for two days? Implement good systems for the operational aspects of your salon and it will run smoothly without you there for a day or two.

7. **Not Being a Control Freak.** The opposite end of the spectrum is true: if you don't exercise enough control, your clients, employees and vendors will take control. Think about it like this: remember in high school when you had a substitute teacher? Don't be the substitute teacher. Instead, be the teacher all the kids liked, listened to and respected.

8. **Not Enough Cash.** Cash flow can be a problem for any small business, salons especially. Some suppliers will ask you to pay up front; others will extend you credit, still others you may have to find your own financing or financial plan in order to buy what they sell. Without enough cash to get things moving (like your product stock, payroll, bills), things often get stuck and stop working entirely. You must budget and allow for emergency funding in order to get over some of the biggest hurdles (the first couple of quarters, the first year, going into the second year).

9. **Lack of Involvement.** Get out there in the community and participate. It's a free or very low cost way to get your name and reputation out there. Participate in charity events, work with local boutiques to put on fashion shows, reach out to groups your clients belong to.

10. **Growing too Fast.** You want to grow, but do so as you're comfortable as an owner, manager and financial partner. When success is on your door and you think expanding is the key to more success, you may want to wait where you are for a while to get used to the workflow and volume of clients, build up some cash reserves and analyze just how you should manage your growth. A little time to reflect will only help you make a better decision.

The biggest mistake we all make is not asking for help. Don't be afraid to ask for help from a mentor, teacher, another successful business owner, the chamber of commerce or anyone whose opinion you respect. You can always take your question to the Internet. A variety of forums, blogs and webpages exist (as do magazines and countless books) to help budding entrepreneurs and startup companies. Check out the sites:

www.small-business-forum.com/

www.smallbusinessbrief.com/forum/

www.openforum.com/

www.startupnation.com/business-forum/

CHAPTER 33

The Money Game

"Creativity comes from zeal to do something. Generally it is to make some money!"

—B. J. Gupta

Money, Money, Who's Got The Money

Today, financing is more difficult that ever to secure. With a shaky economy worldwide, lenders are holding tight to their cash reserves and being even more selective with their loans. That doesn't mean you have to give up your dream of salon ownership, it just means you may have to work harder, and smarter, to get it.

Money puts a strain on things. It limits how far and how fast you can grow as a business and too much or too little can spell disaster (think of the lottery winner horror stories you read about – winning $120 million, then broke, divorced and washed out five years later). But money is out there. From your own savings to small business loans to loans from family members to investors, there's cash available to help you make your dream come true.

But where do you look?

How Deep are Your Pockets?

The idea of taking on a huge debt responsibility and financing all of your startup costs is scary, so look elsewhere. Look at yourself. What can you afford to do to get your business up and running, or close to it, while you secure financing elsewhere?

First, look at what you have available and what you could easily liquidate:

- How much do you have in savings? In checking?
- What percentage of that would you feel comfortable using to self-finance your salon?
- What percentage would you need to hold back to make banks and other lenders feel comfortable about your financial security? (you may want to talk to a loan officer for that one)
- What assets can you sell? Jewelry, cars, antiques, bonds, art, collectibles?
- Do you have any stocks you can leverage or liquidate?
- How much could you draw on an equity line from any real estate you own?

How Deep are Their Pockets

A very popular place to look for startup funding is all around you – your family and friends. They may have cash to provide you with a low interest rate startup loan or an outright cash gift. They may have skills, products or expertise you could use to offset expenses (imagine if your brother-in-law was an electrician and agreed to do wiring for the cost of materials and dinner out? That would save a buck or two). They may have resources and connections you never knew about.

Asking family and friends for money can be awkward, but you can make it easier by presenting them a well-thought-out business plan, as you would for the bank or small business administration. If they see your commitment, your plan and the steps you'll take to execute it, they may be easier to convince.

One outcome of a personal loan from family and friends is the survival of the relationship. How does it work between you if a loan payment is late? If you business fails? If they think you've mismanaged things?

An alternative could be to ask for gifts for your salon. Your friends may be reluctant to give you $100, but four of them may be willing to split the cost of a $400 styling chair or reception desk.

> *Tips*
>
> Before you borrow from a friend or family, you must decide which you need more, the money or the relationship.

Credit Cards

Studies show that the second most popular way to finance a startup (with up to five employees) is with a credit card. Credit cards provide instant money and you can deduct the interest you pay (if you pay any interest at all) if your purchase was business-related.

Take note that credit cards carry a very high interest rate – most are somewhere between 15% and 19%. You only pay interest if you cannot pay the full amount of the bill due, and rates that high add up quickly. All cards offer minimum payments, and, thanks to legislation recently passed, also show a payment schedule based on the minimum amount and a higher amount. If you pay the minimum amount due, you may have more cash in the drawer after paying bills, but that small gain is offset by the massive amounts of interest you're accruing on the credit card debt.

Use a credit card with caution when opening your business. Don't charge more than you can afford to pay off because the high interest rates can put you in a financial tailspin with no way out from the minute you open the doors.

Life Insurance and Retirement Plans

Another source of funding is to take out a loan against the value of a life insurance policy or retirement plan, or drawing money from your retirement plan.

If you hold a whole life insurance policy with at least three years of maturity, you can, in most cases, get a loan against the cash value of the policy. Many insurance companies will lend you up to 90% of your policy's cash value at rates better than those of a bank. Remember, if you go this route, you must keep up with your minimum payments in order to keep the policy in effect.

If you have a 401(k) retirement plan, look into borrowing against the value of the account or at drawing money out of it for use in the business. Some lenders won't offer loans with a 401(k) as collateral, but others will; if this is an option for you, check around and find the best lender. Withdrawing money from your 401(k) carries tax penalties for early withdrawal. Check with the company who facilitates your 401(k) for specific details.

Finding Funding on the Web

The Internet has drastically changed the way some startups go about acquiring financing. A number of sites on the web work with lenders, angel investors, investment funds and groups, small business associations and private venture capitalists to provide assistance in developing a business plan and securing funding.

Look at these sites for more information:

www.bizoffice.com

www.businessfinance.com

www.fundingpost.com

Other sites give you the chance to pitch your idea to the world at large in order to acquire "crowdsourced" funding. That means you make a video telling why people should help you start your salon and people watch the video and give or not. Two main sites facilitate these funding efforts:

www.indiegogo.com

www.kickstarter.com

Both sites have rules governing the types of projects that are eligible, and both handle distribution of funding differently. For instance, if you were trying to raise $10,000 for your salon on kickstarter and you did not reach your goal, the money collected is all refunded to the donors. If you ran the same campaign on indiegogo and only collected $6,358, you would keep that. Both kickstarter and indiegogo keep a percentage of the monies collected as payment for their service, but check with each company for their specific terms.

Bank Loans

Bank loans were difficult to secure before the economic crisis we entered in the mid 2000s; now they're even harder to get.

Generally, banks loan money to companies that are stable and showing profitability or a move toward profitability. Each lender will have different requirements, but most will lend money to businesses with outstanding credit, a three- to five-year track record of improving financial numbers and a solid business plan for the future of the company. Check with your bank, they may have a program for startups or may be able to point you in a good direction.

SBA Financing

The Small Business Administration (SBA) offers government guaranteed loans, usually at rates better than banks. Where many bank loans are five-year terms (you have five years to pay them back), SBA loans are often 10-year loans. This longer payback term is helpful because it reduces the amount you pay each month, which means more cash on hand.

Loan applications with the SBA can be tedious and lengthy, although some SBA programs exist for lower loan amounts – $5,000 to $50,000 – with approval under a month, sometimes even under two weeks.

Check out these two sites for more information:

www.strategiesforsmallbusiness.com

www.sba.gov

Home Equity

If you own your home or any other real estate, you may be able to borrow against the value of the home, take out a second mortgage or refinance the original mortgage. Sometimes you can borrow up to 80% of the home's equity. Remember, if you borrow money against your home or other property, should the business fail and you fail to repay the loan, the bank will foreclose on the home or property.

Leasing

Leasing sources can accommodate all applicants for financing whether you've been in business for 30 years or you're a startup salon. Leasing programs give you the flexibility to finance your furniture, equipment and installation for each. Applications are generally less tedious than with conventional banks.

Once you fill out and submit the application and necessary documents, you'll often have an answer within 72 hours.

If you've been turned down by a bank, leasing companies offer you a great alternative source of financing for large salon expenses, freeing up your cash for other purchases.

Leasing companies like the two below offer personal service (you may get one of the owners on the phone) and reasonable rates for almost all credit situations.

www.questrs.com

www.castletoncapital.com

Government Related Startup Programs

Look for funding from the government, they pump money into a variety of economic development groups and assist business owners based on sex, race, disability, veteran status, geography, the type of business and a dozen other criteria. Federal and state programs are the most common, although your city or municipality may offer financing options as well.

CHAPTER 34

Borrowing from the Bank

"If you know the value of money, go and try to borrow some."

—Benjamin Franklin

As we've pointed out, you have several options for securing financing. Two of the major ways are loans from the bank or a leasing company. In this chapter, we're going to walk you through borrowing from the bank; in the next chapter, we'll look at leasing companies.

How to Get a "Yes" From Your Banker

Preparation is the key if you want the bank's loan officer (or any official who may give you a loan or other funding) to say "Yes" to your loan application. The best way to get the "Yes" you want is by having your paperwork in order and knowing the answers to the most common questions.

Bankers commonly reject a loan for one of five reasons, but it is possible to overcome them and get approval if you follow the suggestions in the next section.

Five Reasons for Loan Rejection

1. No sound business plan
2. Not knowing the exact amount of money you need and how it will be used
3. Not showing the ability to repay the loan
4. Poor credit scores and a bad or shaky credit history
5. Little or no money in the bank or assets to serve as collateral

---

Effectively Informing the Bank About You and Your Salon

Take these key steps to ensure the loan officer is properly informed about your salon.

1. Put together a sound business plan. The plan can be a few pages, but it should be well thought out. The business plan shows the loan officer that you have credibility as the owner and that you're not rushing into something you are unsure of.

2. Be prepared to supply credit references for your business and yourself. You must have a history of repaying distributors and suppliers in full and on time. It's also important that all personal financial obligations – rent, mortgage, student loans, car loans, credit cards and other bills – show a history of good payment practices. If you have a history of slow or late payments, you must have a good explanation in writing or your loan request can be immediately declined.

   Good personal and business credit scores are keys to success.

3. Provide a brief description of the beauty industry, including average and top salaries of stylists, along with the projected annual revenue for your salon. Use industry magazines and specialty publications, like Salon Today's Top 200. Remember, most bankers are unaware that the beauty industry has become a multibillion-dollar profession. The bank must feel confident in the industry, and that, as a part of the industry, your salon is professional and has the potential for growth. Unfortunately, you're battling an industry-wide tarnished reputation brought about by a few individuals who have run their businesses in less than professional ways. Educating your banker or loan official on the profitability of the beauty industry, and your salon in particular, is essential to success.

4. Share your education and experience in running a business, your support structure and other relevant professional details. If you've taken business management classes at the local college, tell the loan officer. If you're enrolled in professional development or business development courses, let them know. Show them your performance record in school and provide them with letters of recommendation from teachers, peers, mentors and business associates.

5. Build a business board to show the bank you're serious. Ask a few friends, family members and business associates to be on your salon's "advisory board." They'll help you make major decisions and lend you their expertise in the business world, marketing, accounting, business management and a number of other areas. Doing this shows the loan officer that you're taking serious steps to ensure your salon's success and longevity.

State Why You Need the Money

When the loan officer asks you how much you'd like to borrow, don't reply with, "How much will you lend me?" It may sound like a funny answer, but trust us, loan officers want to see that you're taking this process seriously and that you have a plan for your funding.

While you're preparing your loan paperwork, you should have an idea of how much money you're looking to borrow. As you developed your business plan, part of your analysis was on startup expenses and projected monthly expenses, so an amount to ask for should be easy to arrive at.

Do Your Numbers Support the Loan Request?

If your business has been at a break-even point (where you're not seeing much of a profit or a loss, but income and expenses are relatively the same) or even losing money, there's still hope, but getting financing won't be easy.

Bankers are trained to make decisions based primarily on a company's ability to generate cash and profit. If you have lost money, you need to be able to explain the losses. In the event of catastrophic events (natural disasters, economic collapse, dire health situations for you or your family), banks offer some degree of leniency and understanding when analyzing your numbers. But, just as they want to know why you saw a loss, they want to know why and how you'll see a profit soon.

The most important thing the bank is looking for is income and profit you are reporting on your tax returns. Hiding income from the IRS is not only illegal, but it will hurt you when applying for a loan. If you tell a loan officer something like "Actually, my tax return doesn't reflect what I really make," you've guaranteed that they will pass on your loan application.

Collateral

Small business owners complain often that lenders lack an adequate understanding of the market value of their businesses' assets like furniture, equipment, inventory and supplies. They're right! Bankers aren't experts on collateral, no matter what is being pledged, and they often lend no more than 80% of the perceived value of the combined real estate and equipment.

You may have personal assets – debt-free automobiles, bank certificates, stocks or other real estate holdings – that could be used to secure the loan. It's a guarantee that the bank will ask you to secure your entire business and will usually look outside the business for other pieces of collateral – that means they're going to look at personal assets.

Personal Guarantees

Most banks won't lend to any business without personal guarantees from the owner or owners. The purpose is to provide a secondary source of repayment in the event the loan goes into default for non-payment. What this means is if you borrow $20,000 and default on the loan, the bank will come after you and your assets to acquire the balance on the loan. If you don't have the cash on hand to pay the balance, they have the legal right to take property equal to the value of the loan.

As a matter of policy, banks ask for personal guarantees from the owner(s). The guarantee not only protects their investment, but shows your commitment to the business.

Applying for a small business loan is not an easy process. The reason it's so difficult is because banks aren't in the business of losing money, they want to make back their investment, in time and capital, from you repaying your loan. They're not looking to make risky investments; that's why you need to have your financial paperwork in order and know the answers to common questions.

Using Your Home as Collateral

Many first time business owners are so sure they'll succeed, they're willing to wager a lot on it, namely their house. If you own your home, it's undoubtedly your biggest piece of collateral and while it will certainly help you secure a loan, if your gamble doesn't pay off, you won't just lose your business, you'll lose your home.

Banks have always been conservative, but the ongoing economic slowdown has them behaving more cautiously when lending money, especially to new businesses. They feel that the risk associated with financing a new business is so high that they'll ask personal collateral to tie to the loan – a 401(k), life insurance policy or automobile or boat is good, but a house, that's great.

If you're considering pledging your home as collateral, be aware of what could happen if your business should fail. We are sure the worst feeling in the world would be for you to get a phone call one day letting you know that your home is being seized because your business has failed and the loan has come due.

That's one way of finding out the harsh reality of putting your home up as collateral.

What if you were at home one day and a local Sherriff's Deputy showed up at your door with a warrant letting you know your home is being seized because of a default on your loan payments? Now you have no business and no home.

Before you take the step to put your home on the table as collateral, think through the worst-case scenarios and let that help guide your decision.

All that about the bank calling or the Sheriff coming by isn't an exaggeration, although it is at one extreme end of the spectrum for the banks. What generally happens is that the bank identifies that your loan is in trouble and beings to take steps to work with you on a repayment plan that allows you to keep your home. Remember, banks are in the business of lending money, not owning homes, they don't want to take your home any more than you don't want them to. As collateral, your home is a last resort, but banks will, when pushed past their financial pain point, take ownership of the home.

Currently, the value of business assets amounts to somewhere between $.10 and $.20 on the dollar when auctioned off. After the entire salon is auctioned off, the bank will look to the borrowers to settle the remaining debt. That's when the home you pledged as collateral comes into play.

When a bank accepts a home as collateral in a loan, they put a lien on the home for the entire value of the loan amount borrowed, even in that amount is more than the homeowner's equity. The bank's philosophy is that, in time, the equity will increase through the appreciation of the home over the life of the loan. The bank's lien will be a secondary lien behind the primary mortgage holder.

If your business does fail, that doesn't mean the bank automatically takes the home. As we said, they will usually work with you to set up a payment plan that gives them their money and lets you keep the home. The auction of the salon's assets will cover some of the costs, but you, the loan holder, are responsible for the remainder. If you can come up with enough money to settle your debt, you can get out from under the loan and keep your home. In today's salon world, due to cheap import furniture flooding the market, your equipment could be worth very little as collateral. A premium product will bring a premium price when used as collateral.

The B Word

Bankruptcy. It's not a thought any of us like to entertain, but in dire cases it's an option to consider.

You may have heard the phrases "Chapter 11 Bankruptcy," or maybe "Chapter 7" or "Chapter 13;" these are types of bankruptcy that are used for personal or business debt restructuring. Under most of the "chapters" of bankruptcy (the "chapters" refer to sections of the bankruptcy legal code), borrowers or debtors have the opportunity to settle their debts in either court-ordered or legally mandated ways.

Bankruptcy is actually the most common course of action borrowers take. After trying everything to save their business and home, many feel they don't have another option and file for bankruptcy.

At the point when bankruptcy is filed, it's usually too late for a small business or a startup to recover (larger corporations may file for certain chapters of bankruptcy in order to restructure debt and survive it) – the business loan is in default, the mortgage is unpaid, every personal asset has been leveraged to squeeze the last dollar out. By now, it's time to throw in the towel and consult with a bankruptcy attorney or another bankruptcy expert about a possible course of action.

We didn't say all this to scare you, but to let you see the situation for what it is.

Most banks speak to their business owners on a regular basis. In many cases, business owners who have a business loan from the bank are required to provide financial reports to the lender (usually it's in the form of tax returns). If you have honest, open communication with the bank, you can let them know of any trouble you're encountering and see if there's something you can do to stop it before it turns ugly and costs you your business or home.

If you see you're having difficulty, make an appointment with your accountant to review the business' books and approach the bank with a series of plans to help you keep your business.

It's true that going into business has some great rewards, but it's also true that it can be hard and scary at times. Not all of us are going to have a successful business; in fact, some of us may have two, three or four unsuccessful businesses before they find the one that brings success. Business ownership is a gamble, be careful before you put up your home as collateral – that's the absolute last resort.

CHAPTER 35

Leasing for the Life of Your Business

"Money can't buy happiness, it can, however, rent it."

—Anonymous

Have you ever heard of sweat equity? It's the labor that you put into your own projects. As you move closer to opening or revamping your salon, you're going to invest a lot of sweat equity into getting it right.

In addition to sweat equity, you'll be investing a lot of finances into your business. Savings, loans, gifts from family and friends, sure, all of these will give you a little of what you need, but where do you turn when the bank says "No" to your loan application? How do you pay for the fixtures, equipment and installation? Where do you turn?

You turn to a lease finance company.

For years, distributors and manufacturers in the beauty industry have known about furniture and equipment leasing as a financing option, but only in the last 15 years or so have smaller salons taken advantage of this type of financing.

Here are 10 reasons why you, as a salon owner, should use leasing as a financial tool in place of conventional bank financing.

Bank vs. Lease Finance Company

In order to be approved at your local bank, the applicant must submit three years of personal and corporate tax returns with a completed loan application. The corporate returns must show a profit in order or the bank to consider lending any money to the business. Leasing companies require an application that is typically reviewed the same day it is received and can be approved for up to $75,000. The process is quite different from traditional, tedious bank loans. In fact, more than 90% of salons wouldn't qualify for a conventional bank loan in today's business environment because most fail to show a profit (or show a very small profit when they do). For a lease finance company to consider you a good candidate, you need to meet minimum qualifications, but a lot of the decision rests on your credit score. We cannot emphasize enough: You must have a great credit score.

Startup Financing

Without a minimum of two years of continual operation, most banks won't consider extending credit to your salon. So how are you supposed to finance a startup?

Typically the only lender willing to extend financing to startup salon businesses are those with a niche expertise in a particular line of equipment or industry. Therefore, if you are a new salon owner, leasing may be your best bet and may well be the most competitive option for obtaining new furniture and equipment. Your furniture and equipment sales representatives will be able to help you identify a company that fits your needs.

Establish Business Credit

To be considered for a business loan, your business needs to have a credit record. Lease financing establishes that credit as you make your on-time payments. As your business grows, you'll need to acquire new equipment and furniture to meet increased demand and fill the salon space. By establishing your credit with a lease company, it becomes easier to purchase your next piece of furniture or equipment or expand, relocate or remodel your salon.

Home vs. Equipment

The only collateral pledged on an equipment lease is the equipment. There's a 0% chance of losing your home due to payment default. Lease companies don't ask for personal collateral, which leaves you, your family, your possessions and the life you've built out of the frying pan if your business didn't go as planned.

Quick Turnaround

If opening your own business or your remodel project is like most, it will run over budget, which can exhaust your cash supply or leave you short handed, which makes opening on time and fully equipped, stocked and staffed a difficult prospect. Equipment lease financing lets you avoid a lengthy approval process so you can get everything ordered and installed in a matter of weeks. Upon receipt of your credit application and lease quote (how much you'd like to borrow), most lease companies will respond with approval, rejection or a request for additional information within 24 hours.

Conserve Your Money

Lease financing allows you to conserve your money, which you can utilize elsewhere in your business. Leasing offers you a predictable payment to fit into your budget. The fixed repayment price won't fluctuate like many traditional business loans, and the interest rate will stay the same for the life of the lease.

Down Payment

Equipment lease financing does not require a large down payment, which is the normal case for traditional loans. You can expect to put down 10% or less of the equipment lease as a security deposit.

Tax Advantages

Leasing offers you the ability to write off lease payments. Depending on the terms of your lease payment agreement, you may be able to subtract the payment as an expense for the life of the agreement. A bank loan doesn't offer this write-off. Take advantage of the recently modified IRS Section 179, which enables businesses to write off thousands of dollars of leased equipment every year.

Avoid Obsolescence

Technology and designs are always changing, including new equipment for processing color, display cases, salon software and other tools you need. Why should you be stuck with outdated equipment that puts you at a competitive disadvantage? With equipment financing, you can obtain the new technology and keep your salon out in front of the competition.

Going Out of Business

In the event of default, the lease agreement usually indicated the lessor will repossess the leased equipment and resell it for fair market value. This is different from a bank loan. Default on that and the bank simply holds an auction and asks for the balance due. They have no interest in reselling equipment or wanting you to succeed.

Today there are a handful of lease companies (Quest Resources and Castleton Capital, among others) that focus on your niche – the beauty industry. You may find it easier to discuss your salon's needs with a lease company that has an ongoing relationship with equipment and furniture manufacturers and distributors.

Above everything else, you'll enjoy the process of working with a company who has an understanding of the beauty industry as well as the needs of salons similar to yours. They have the knowledge, passion and resources at their disposal to help set you up for success.

When Lease Financing Equipment or Retail Furniture, Remember to Ask:

- Do you own the equipment at the end of the term?
- Are you responsible to have insurance on the leased equipment?
- Who maintains the equipment?
- Can you give the equipment away or sell it at the end of the term?
- Who is responsible for the tax on the sale of the equipment?

CHAPTER 36

Transition Time

"I always liked the story of Noah's Ark and the ide of starting anew by rescuing the things you like and leaving the rest behind."

—Zach Braff

After the months of planning, building and installing, your salon is almost finished and your move-in date is on top of you. What do you do if you are currently working at another salon? How do you make your exit? If you work for yourself and are expanding or branching into a different career, this chapter will have some helpful information; but for those of you transitioning from one job to another, this chapter is for you. In this chapter, we'll answer questions like:

- How do you transition?
- When do you tell the salon owner?
- Do you tell your current employer and hope for the best?
- When do you tell your clients?
- How do you hire your staff?
- When do you start promoting your salon?

This chapter will guide you through all of these questions and give you suggestions and things to consider.

If you are thinking about your transition out of your current job, then that means the lease is done and you need to start planning your business model. If your salon won't be ready for four to six months because of construction, then we recommend that you tell NO ONE! That means no bragging about it on Facebook, blogging about it (you can blog about it, but publish them as you're right on top of your opening date), giving interviews to the media about it or any other thing that will draw attention to you. Tell only your closest and most trusted confidants to keep it under wraps as long as possible. Of course, discuss everything with your significant other or business partner going in on the business, but other than that, tell no one.

We have seen many future salon owners tell a few of their trusted clients and, after a few weeks, a client may slip and say something to the salon owner or another hairdresser. Believe it or not, the average person only picks up 11 percent of a person's conversation, so the odds they don't hear you say, "Don't tell anyone, but I'm opening my own salon" are slim.

The best strategy is to build your client list slowly and surely over a longer period. Look at your regular client list. Who would you like to take to your new salon? Which clients come in more frequently? Spend more per visit? Bring their family? Refer you to friends? Which ones would you want to sit in your chair again? Make notes of their styles, color formulas, product preferences and other information that may help you provide them with their ideal salon experience.

Once you've made your list, begin to quietly gather email addresses and telephone numbers. Don't tell them about the new salon yet, just let them know you're updating your contact files for future promotions. You have to be discreet when you do this. If the salon owner sees you gathering this information, they will get suspicious. If they get suspicious, they may find out about the salon and terminate your position immediately.

> **NOTE**
>
> One way to gather contact information quickly and quietly is to collect business cards from your clients who have one.

If your salon is close to your existing workplace (or even if it's across town in a high-traffic, high-visibility area, which we know it will be, you took our advice after all), we recommend that you put paper in the windows in the front of the store, keep your front door locked and have your construction crew use the back entrance. If the salon owner you work for suspects competition, he or she will stop by to see who is opening up, what services they are offering, and snoop around to find out as much as possible. You want to be strategic and stay hidden as long as possible. It's only natural that your current salon owner will want to find out the competing salon in their backyard.

You do not want your owner to walk into the location while it's under construction; they might tell a construction worker or the general contractor that they're looking for work and would like to get in touch with the new owner. The crew may not realize the implications and say your name or give your telephone number because they think they are helping you to get a new employee. Have a conversation with your construction crews about this situation. "If someone comes asking about the owner and looking for work, collect their information and put it here for me to collect." Remember, the owner can research the county or state tax records, corporate filings, business license records and a dozen other places to find out who may be opening the salon; so, make the mailing address a post office box number or your attorney's office until you open, that makes it much more difficult to trace.

> **When do you tell the current salon owner?**
>
> We have seen many stylists tell the salon owner months in advance about opening their own salon. Since they felt more like a friend than an employee, they mistakenly thought that the owner would be very happy for them. Unless the salon is located more than 20 miles away, you become a threat to your employer. In most cases, you will be immediately fired.

If your current boss finds out about the new salon, they may terminate you on the spot. The next thing you know, you are trying to scramble to find a place to work and keep your existing clientele. The salon owner will try to take your clients away from you, not tell them where you have gone, book them with another stylist and keep as many of your clients as possible. So, you need to tell your employer when you are prepared to leave. Whenever possible, wait until the last minute. They may say, "Stay until you are open." But, in most cases, you are not only the competition, but you will take your clients and possibly other stylists or providers with you. Be very careful.

When do you tell your fellow stylists? It is a very difficult question. Again, if you are months away from opening, tell no one. Your news will leak out if the "wrong" person overhears a conversation about what you are doing. The next thing you know, you will be called into the owner's office and fired. You can put your whole plan in jeopardy if you are let go from your current, income-producing job before you are ready. We would wait until you are a few weeks from opening and prepared to leave before saying anything.

> **Tips**
>
> What will you do when you own your own salon and your top stylist steps in to tell you they're leaving to start their own salon? How would you like them to handle it? That's how you should handle your exit.

How do you hire your staff? The first person you need to hire and look for is your front desk professional or a salon manager. That person will help you hire and keep you out of the limelight before you open. There will be a number of tasks that need to be done before you open, and the right hire will have the expertise to help you execute your plans effectively. This person will be very helpful while you are still working to produce revenue. It is very important that you get along with this person, have the same philosophy, and understand the path and the culture you want to create. For salons with a retail focus, it's also important that your hire be familiar with your salon software (or that you give them training), retail pricing strategies, have a friendly demeanor so they can speak with vendors if necessary and understand the way your retail supports the salon side and vice versa.

The front desk professional or salon manager is an investment. As soon as you hire this person, they are going to want a salary. Try to be creative with them, but figure it into your budget. One option is to enter into a profit sharing situation, similar to a commission for a salesperson. Offer them a base salary (that's a living wage) and a percentage of net profits (profits after all expenses are paid). This incentivizes them to sell more, think strategically about retail sales and salon bookings and gives them a stake in the salon without you actually giving up part of ownership. Now, you are ready to look for staff.

You can find stylists in salons, but be careful. In a small town or when your salon is in close proximity to your existing salon, gossip spreads like a bad fire. It is always great to bring someone on board with a full book, but be careful of the commission they are asking for and be careful of the consequences. You don't want to open your salon and have a community of stylists and salon owners ignoring your requests for help or advice because you "stole" their top stylists.

Another way to hire your staff is to go to an industry school to find them. L'Oreal-affiliated schools offer excellent education and are a viable source for finding newly trained students. First, find the school, get to know the manager, and find out the best students graduating. Bring in friends and family to try out the newly graduated student. If you feel this person does quality work, it's like finding a diamond in the rough. Be aware that when hiring stylists fresh out of school you're getting an employee with no experience in the business world. This is an opportunity to mold them into a model employee, but it will take a while. You may have to live with some immature behavior until they get with your program.

The best part in all of this is that new graduates will be open to understand and be receptive to the business culture and atmosphere you want to create. Also, you can start the student at 40 percent commission as an apprentice. Then, gradually work them up to a higher percentage after a 6-month period. Since new graduates don't have followings, it is important that you budget more money for marketing and advertising to get new clients into your salon.

Let's say you are opening a salon far away from your existing place of work. How do you find staff? Well, one way is to place postcards in all the strip malls that are close to your location, stating that you are opening and looking for stylists, colorists, nail techs, and massage therapists. You will get some phone calls; there are always people who are ready for a move or unhappy in their present salon for one reason or another.

Although it may seem like a good idea at first, going into a busy salon to seek out and lure the superstars away from their current job and salon is not advisable. Just like you have a dream of salon ownership, your fellow salon owners have that same dream. Find ways to attract job seekers to you, rather than hunting them down and pulling them from other salons. Acquiring people this way can lead to a slew of problems. If you think of someone coming into your salon and pulling away the people that you've invested in and worked hard to acquire, you would be upset and angry.

Do the hard work to find qualified candidates; it will pay off. Stick with schools, word-of-mouth, print classifieds and online classifieds as well.

Craigslist is a great place to start with online classifieds. If you look on Craigslist right now, you will find a ton of ads for beauty salon employment (and equipment). It's recommended that you create an email that is just for use with your Craigslist account and employment ads. Unfortunately, the one issue with Craigslist is the amount of spam that you will receive. Regardless, it is still a great way to place free ads about your salon's job openings.

Now that you've successfully managed to exit the salon you worked in without involving the police (hopefully), it's time to set up your retail and color department.

But not so fast.

Your old boss' relationship with their distributor/manufacturer could make this process simple or easy. We talked about relationships in Chapter 26 and the importance of that chapter comes into play moving forward.

Hopefully you can develop a strong ongoing relationship with your distributors. I n this economic climate, your request to sell anyone's product should be relatively easy and they should welcome you and your salon with open arms, provide there isn't a territorial exclusivity or proximity agreement in place with another salon in the area.

If you plan on hiring any of your coworkers from your previous job, remember to hire ones who use and are educated on the products you plan to sell. This will help you do two things: sell effectively and maintain reliable retail clients.

When Deciding on a Product Brand for Backbar or Retail, You Must Remember That:

1. Your prior employer may have an exclusive right to a product within a territory (usually a radius or zip code) or a strong enough relationship to keep you out. Loyalty is big in the beauty industry and some suppliers may be reluctant to ruin an existing, reliable and profitable relationship to gain a small, upstart salon.

2. Hiring and training staff may come down to what products you use and supply in your salon.

3. When making a retailing decision to sell a product that your clients can afford, don't price yourself out of the neighborhood.

THE PROS KNOW

"Leaving any salon where you work is not easy. I suggest being very upfront and honest with your owner and/or manager because you never know when your paths may cross again. It is not often well received when you tell them you plan on leaving. The process should always be done with integrity. Hopefully your employee will respond in the same way. I know that I've never fired someone who told me they were leaving if they explained what they were going to do and did so in a professional manner."

Joni Jarrell
Designer Line Hair Studio, Ocala, FL

CHAPTER 37

Booth Rental

"The duty of the tenant is to pay the rent. The duty of the landlord is to collect it."

—Robert Dangoor

Most salons work in one of two ways – the salon hires stylists and they are employees of the salon; or the salon rents booth space to stylists. Both operations have up sides and down sides, but renting booth space to stylists can be another great income stream for your salon.

Types of Booth Rental Operations

Booth-Rental Salon with All Private Rooms

A salon with rooms to rent is the Beverly Hills of booth rental. Each stylist has their own room to treat as their studio. In every room is a mini salon – styling chair, shampoo station, dryer, phone system and maybe even a computer terminal for future bookings. For stylists (or cosmetologists, massage therapists, colorists, nail techs, et cetera), this type of rental can be a great learning opportunity and give them a taste of what it's like to run their own salon. Which can be dangerous for you as the salon owner – you don't want to become a farm where stylists come to learn the business then leave to start their own salon.

Creating Your Own Booth Renting Operation

Creating a booth-renting salon is not the standard practice in the industry, though some salons have seen a lot of success with this model and more are making the switch to this type of operation. We've worked with several successful operations and understand how to create a profitable salon environment. Here's a brief description of the startup costs and equipment needed to open this type of salon.

1. **Construction**
   - Increased electric – you'll need outlets in every room and a more complex wiring system

- Increased plumbing and an upgraded hot water system (like a tankless water heater) to outfit each room with a shampoo station
- Communication wiring – for the phone lines, internet ports and credit card machines in each booth
- Air conditioning – each space will need to be air conditioned and have some degree of control over their temperature
- Building materials like lumber and drywall – you're building several rooms, you need to construct walls, put sheetrock on them and finish them out with molding, doors, et cetera
- Flooring – you'll want a durable flooring system for each room
- Lighting – each room must have adequate lighting
- Bathrooms – you may want to expand your bathroom to add a second stall or install a second bathroom to accommodate increased client traffic
- Painting – with more walls, you need more paint to cover them. This increases costs in labor and material
- Carpentry – someone has to build it, now they're building even more
- Break room
- Laundry room

2. Equipment

In every room you'll need:

- Sinks and backwash units
- Dryer chairs
- Reception chairs
- Hydraulic styling chairs
- Storage cabinets
- Workstations

In addition, you'll need a front of house reception desk and retail display area

3. Costs

- Upfront construction will be much more expensive
- Equipment costs are significantly more expensive – now you're buying twice as much equipment as a traditional salon
- Deposits for rent are higher because you're in a larger space
- Legal fees are higher – you'll need to create contracts for renters
- Insurance premiums are larger and liability increases
- Salary for front desk person and salon manager

The booth-rental salon allows you to be a salon owner without the nuisance of running and managing staff. You can pull back to work on larger issues like marketing, retail management and establishing your salon as a brand.

In a booth-rental salon, you become the landlord and are responsible for your tenants. Although this may seem easier than working the floor and running the business, keep in mind that your renters will have demands and personalities you must deal with, and there's the added stress of keeping the booths rented.

Other things to be aware of for booth-rent salons

- Once you're at 100% capacity (fully rented), your income is capped and you'll have to identify other revenue streams

- Expenses go up when renting – expect higher utility bills and supply orders than you initially planned for

- Turnover is higher than in a normal salon

- Maintenance costs are greater

- Hours of operation are longer

Open Booth Renting – No Rooms

This looks like your traditional salon and, to your clients, behaves just like a normal salon. Most of the time, all expenses are paid by the salon owner (that means utilities, supplies, laundry, et cetera are your responsibility) unless there is an agreement with booth renters to pay for shampoo assistants and product costs.

Owning the salon and renting it out has good and bad points.

The positive is that your overhead is covered and you, as the owner, are behind the chair making a good income while the rent on the remaining chairs covers all expenses and puts a little money into the salon's account.

The negative is that your income is limited to what you can make. If your renters leave, this can leave a hole in your income that's sometimes hard to fill.

Every situation is different, but the bottom line is to do your projections and see what your profits could be. By doing your homework on booth rental versus traditional salon operations, you can enter into your business having made a decision you can live with.

Booth Rental and Retail Sales

Remember the following:

1. A well-written contract between the salon and landlord or salon owner and booth renter will help everyone understand the relationship and their individual

responsibilities. The exact wording regarding retail is important in a booth rent agreement. Unless the sub-lease specifically contains a non-compete clause, it is legal for the booth renter to sell retail that competes directly with the salon. Our advice: spend the money and have a lawyer review sublease contracts for your booth renters to make sure all your bases are covered.

2. Be careful about the way you pay booth renters for selling retail. If you pay them a commission on their sales, you are coming dangerously close (or may be crossing the line) to a traditional employee/employer relationship. Depending on the laws in your area, this relationship can be created by anything from a commission structure to the ways funds are distributed to the rules the salon owner puts on the booth renter regarding how they run their retail business. We recommend a non-compete and supplier agreement with booth renters and then, as the salon, supplying the retail products to booth renters at a slight markup (something like 10% over wholesale, which leaves plenty of margin for them to profit from the sale).

3. Booth renters who have the choice to retail their preferred product without interference ay be subjecting customers to retail overload by offering too many choices at too many pricepoints. We recommend controlling this as much as possible.

From the booth renter's perspective, the relationship can be tricky as well. Depending on the relationship with the salon owner and the retail setup, customers buying retail may:

- Be confused when seeing products as they walk in the salon that are different than what booth renters are selling.
- Buy products at the front desk, assuming they are buying from the stylist.
- Buy products at the front desk because you don't have a credit card machine.
- Buy products from the front desk because you don't have the space for retail products in your area.

The benefit of owning a booth-rental salon is not having the worries of managing stylists, nail technicians, barbers and spa therapist. There are many people who love the business model of not having employees and collecting rent every month. The down side is that the income is the rent you collect each month, which means you're limited financially by the number of booths available and rented. Many owners turn to other income streams, like retail.

Tips

Renting a booth or joining a salon suites can be a great place for you to learn your business before opening a salon.

When Renting A Booth

Both booth-rental salon owners and renters need to realize one thing: you're not just renting the chair or table where you work, you're renting every square inch of your allotted space. In order to be profitable, you must use every part of it to maximize sales. A little extra shelving; a simple, attractive display; or the right signage can boost sales and profits for everyone involved.

Pay a visit to smaller, successful salons and spas. How do they make use of their space? Do they exploit every opportunity for sales, as we pointed out in the Retail Zones section? What are they doing that works? Even though space is a premium in small salons, notice that the most successful ones display more than just one or two or a product. Why would you do this when space is so precious? Because people are reluctant to take the last item. More stock out entices buyers to buy.

Maximizing sales can be as easy as prominently displaying the prices and promotions on your products, tools and services. Female customers (more so than male customers) are reluctant to ask the price of an item, avoid this by having everything clearly labeled with the price.

Remember that if you rent a booth, you can't sell retail if you aren't there, which means less profit for you and the salon owner. The salon owner isn't going to sell products on your behalf, so be sure to sell, sell, sell.

Working in or Owning a Booth-rental Salon Can Complicate Your Relationship with Distributors/Manufacturers. Keep in Mind:

- It may be difficult for vendors to locate your business or pay you a visit if you're not there full time.

- Manufacturers offer education, and if there isn't someone at the front desk or a manager or owner around to arrange sessions, the entire salon may miss out on educational opportunities.

- Buying sporadically will not give you the necessary wholesale discounts to sell products at a competitive price.

- Not having a strong relationship with vendors will result in buying everything COD (Cash On Delivery) rather than with a credit line.

- Not buying at a high enough volume or frequency may mean that you're charged for marketing material like signage, giveaways and branded bags.

- It can be very difficult to establish your own brand and relationships with national brands.

CHAPTER 38

Building Your Business to Sell

"A successful man is one who can lay a firm foundation with the bricks others have thrown at him."

—David Brinkley

Ok, we admit it, this whole book is about building your business to sell retail products, but this time we mean building your business into something you can sell to another entrepreneur when it's time to transition into the next phase of your life, be it retirement, travel, family or another business. After reading this chapter, we hope you understand some of the basics of putting a value on your business and developing it into something another entrepreneur would want to buy.

You should always have a grasp on the value of your salon. If you needed to borrow money for the business quickly, transfer your company to a family member, sell a percentage to a deserving employee or sell the business outright, what value would you place on it? Many business owners think the value is simply a multiple of earnings, but it's far more than that.

Perhaps the best way to gain an understanding of the value of your salon is to look at it through the eyes of a potential buyer. This will enable you to identify the key characteristics that influence the value of your salon. Speak with your accountant for a general idea of the growth potential, current and historical state of the salon's financial situation, all of which will give you an idea of its future worth.

Here are a few guidelines to keep in mind during the course of selling your business:

Placing a value on your business can be a challenging project. With good financial records, a bank officer, commercial realtor, business broker, business coach or accounting team can help you accurately determine the value of your retail salon.

Serving Niche Markets

Trying to be everything to everyone can cloud your vision for the company and expose it to competition from specialty salons around you. Instead, position your company with a unique selling proposition and establish your salon as a market leader. Your salon should be known for delivering the latest trends, best color, a luxurious experience, and a full service suite. Focus on becoming the best in a class, then expand, don't try to do it all at once.

In a good market, you are often better owning 60% of a niche than 1% of a broader market. Niche players have a sharp focus on a specific product, service or type of customer. Niche business owners know their target client inside and out –what they need and, more importantly, what they want – and deliver products and services tailored to them.

A prospective buyer for your salon will look at the niche you serve. They'll look for ways to gain more market share in the niche and ways to spread into related niches. If you can establish a solid client base and a reputation within your chosen niche, it adds a tremendous amount of value to your business.

Sell Consumable Products

This book is all about retail sales in your salon and we cannot stress enough that you need to sell a product to your clients that they will use, love, run out of and come back to buy more. Showing a potential buyer a steady stream of sales numbers makes you more valuable. And it's not just buyers who would want to see these sales numbers. Think about applying for a loan or industry award. Both places will ask, "Why do you deserve to receive this? What can you show me to prove your growth?" Strong sales numbers, an increase in revenue and a solid presence in the retail market give you a good case for a higher valuation for buyers or loan officers, and are a great argument for industry awards.

Build an Organization

A business that relies on one or two people is worth less to a potential buyer or bank than a company with a strong management team. Buyers don't like a one-man operation. You may be the best colorist or stylist and have built a name for you and your salon, but when you leave, so does the best colorist or stylist and a buyer is left with nothing but a few clients who will stick around.

Building a larger salon doesn't mean you have to relinquish control over every detail in the business, you just have to learn to delegate and allow other leaders to emerge within the business. Sure, this can be a long process and can become more complex and difficult to manage, but a good mentor or business coach can help you with some of the finer points and get your organization running smoothly. The payoff is when you want to step away and sell – now your salon can run without you and is far more valuable to a buyer.

Maintain Credible Financial Statements

Financial statements give you a look at the state of the company at a glance – assets, liabilities, profit and loss, sales, income, revenue and more. A true financial statement will give a buyer the confidence to make a decision on the value of your salon. This means no fudging the numbers, no forgetting to file a tax form or input sales figures into your accounting software. It means being on top of things at all times.

Profits + Sales = Higher Price

Projecting the value of a company that is always up and down in their income is difficult and potential buyers will place a lower value on companies with sales figures that aren't consistent.

A salon with steady sales figures is better. But the best is one with steady sales and a demonstrated profit increase over time. It's important to keep sales as consistent as possible and identify opportunities to fill in the valleys in your sales figures.

Low Overhead and No Debt

Many salons make themselves impossible to sell at any price because the debts exceed the gross value (total value before debt is accounted for) of the business. If your business is upside down like this, know that potential buyers and potential lenders will look at your salon and give it a much lower value than the same business with a better debt to value ratio.

If you are able to sell your business, the outstanding debt would be deducted from the gross purchase price. That leaves some sellers with a small profit and others with no profit at all. The key is to run a tight ship, keep costs under control, develop a niche and provide the products and services that nice wants, keep growth and expansion under control and stay focused on your goals (which you are constantly evaluating).

A Potential Buyer May Buy Your Salon Because:
- Profit from recurring retail sales are a big percentage of your business.
- They are familiar with the retail brands you carry.
- You are making more profit selling retail than services.
- You are not the biggest earner in the salon (meaning your salon and the renters or employees there carry the burden of earning).
- All of your sales are recorded and accounted for in your software and your accounting is in order.
- Your staff is professional and courteous.
- You salon has a solid online reputation on Facebook, Google, Yelp, Foursquare and other social media platforms.

CHAPTER 39

Timeline

"Life is all about timing…the unreachable becomes reachable, the unavailable becomes available, the unattainable…attainable. Have the patience, wait it out. It's all about timing."

—Stacey Charter

ONE YEAR (or more) BEFORE OPENING

- Look at the pros and cons of owning and operating your own salon
- Decide if you are ready
- Take the entrepreneurial self-test
- Analyze the market to see if and where your salon would fit
- Will you buy an existing salon or start your own?
- Decide if you will rent booths

BUYING AN EXISTING SALON

- Analyze the operation
- Review financials
- Create a spreadsheet with projections and debt ratios
- Create a budget
- Make an offer to purchase
- Remodel the salon
- Hire an architect and contractor
- Determine your list priorities for coordination and timing
- Begin your transformation weekend

STARTING A NEW SALON, SPA OR BARBERSHOP

- Choose a business structure
- Name your salon
- Hire a lawyer
- Gather/apply for:

EIN (Employer Identification Number)

Articles of Incorporation

Resolution

Identification

- Pick a location for your new salon
- Complete the startup expense worksheet
- Work on your new business checklist: business plan and mission statement
- SECURE STARTUP FUNDS!!
- Negotiate your lease
- Find an equipment designer and architect
- Price your salon furniture
- Find your contractor
- Obtain licenses and permits:

    EIN (Employer Identification Number)

    Articles of Incorporation

    Resolution

    Identification

    Initial deposit

- Set up a business checking account
- Plan your signage
- Choose the colors of your salon
- Obtain business insurance for opening day of business
- Hire a bookkeeper and/or an accountant
- Design and develop web presence and determine social marketing strategy
- Decide on computers and software for your salon
- Choose a business phone system
- Write your employee manual
- Design and develop a salon menu
- Set up online promotions
- Choose which retail products to sell and meet with appropriate vendors
- Begin to hire

WITHIN SIX MONTHS OF OPENING

- Plan salon promotions and loyalty programs
- Meet with vendors and suppliers of retail products and fixtures to narrow down your selections
- Discuss finance options with vendors

- Discreetly begin the hiring process
- Study sales cycles and ads of competitors to gather ideas for your advertising

WITHIN THREE MONTHS OF OPENING

- Arrange for salon promotions and loyalty programs (negotiate with vendors, decide if you need loyalty cards, etc.)
- Finalize retail selection
- Place initial orders (time frame may be closer to one month depending on the vendor)
- Contact a web designer to help you set up a website for your salon

WITHIN ONE MONTH OF OPENING

- Train staff on computer software and hardware
- Double check all permits and inspections

WITHIN TWO OR THREE WEEKS OF OPENING

- The controversial exit
- Meet with staff at the new salon to train them on company policies and procedures
- Preparing for the open house

AFTER OPENING

- Successful retail in year one
- Surviving the first year—what to expect and how to adjust
- Identify opportunities to exploit – new niches, expansion, new hires
- Build your business to sell

THE PROS KNOW

Alisha Wendt from Blush Haus of Beaute in Wilmington, NC, had some great parting words:

"Most salons are run and operated like a gas station. Most gas stations make their money on in the convenience store. Selling services isn't as important for the bottom line as you'd think. Building the income from the convenience store side – the retail side – of the business is essential and makes them profitable."

"Yes, service is important, but if you want to eventually sell your business, you have to build your convenience store business – that's your retail!"

"All boats rise with the tide and if your stylists sell retail, your salon will rise above the others and you salon will be worth more when the time comes to sell."

Special Thanks

Jeff and Eric would like to especially thank and acknowledge Patrick Parenty, L'Oreal, and their divisions for supporting Ready, Set, Go! and helping to make this one-of-a-kind publication a reality.

Contributors & Resources

Jeff Grissler, Quest Resources, Salon Equipment Financing (jgrissler@questrs.com). www.questrs.com

John Harms, President/Founder, Harms Software (Millennium). www.harms-software.com

Guy Wadas, National Sales Director, Integrity Payment Systems. www.integritypaymentsystems.com

Facebook Friends

Thank you for providing your stories and allowing us to share That's What They Say.*
Follow Jeff Grissler and Eric David Ryant on Facebook.

Image Sources

Takara Belmont – www.takarabelmont.com

Peter Millard Designs – www.millard-design.com

Rick Golden, Takara Belmont Design Specialist – rgolden@takarabelmont.com

Jeff Holmes, Takara Belmont Regional Manager – jholmes@takarabelmont.com

European Touch Pedicure Spas – www.europeantouch.com

Blush Haus of Beaute – www.blushhob.com

Salon Centric Equipment Division – www.saloncentric.com

Editing and Production

B. Jason Frye, Writing and Editing
Teakettle Junction Productions
4642 Middlesex Road
Wilmington, North Carolina 28405

Interior Layout and Cover Design
Robin Krauss
Linden Design
www.lindendesign.biz

Business Resources

- Salon Consulting
- Design Layout and Plans
- School – Class Education
- Equipment Procurement
- Business Education

Jeff Grissler – jgrissler@questrs.com
Eric Ryant – ericryant@gmail.com

Quest Resources

Beauty Equipment Finance Specialists
We make your salon dreams possible.
www.questrs.com
800-449-0777

Follow Jeff and Eric on Facebook.

Visit us on the web at:
www.readysetgobooks.com
www.salonresourceguide.com

*Quotes provided via Facebook were offered freely by salon owners and without obligation or compensation from Ready, Set, Go! Publishing, its authors, contributors, or endorsers. Quotes used in this book follow "fair use" practices with proper attribution given to those who submitted comments. When content is offered via a public domain, such as Facebook, it means that those posting or commenting are allowing their posts or comments to be shared, used or accessed by people on and off of Facebook.